T0357666

"Topher Endress alternates his de
reflections on accompanying people
relationships with chapters written by
John, who describes his own adjustment to quadriplegia caused by a
hiking accident. This book highlights both the grittiness and sublime
and can be read by anyone."

—**BILL GAVENTA**, Founder and Director Emeritus,
Institute on Theology and Disability,
and author of *Disability and Spirituality:
Recovering Wholeness*

"Endress offers a deeply moving and theologically rich reflection on
the intersections of disability, caregiving, and faith. Through poignant
storytelling and thoughtful analysis, *Accompanying Disability* challenges us to reimagine the sacred roles of accompaniment and care,
revealing God's presence in the complexities of everyday life. This is
essential reading for anyone seeking a nuanced and compassionate
exploration of caregiving as both a spiritual and transformative act."

—**JOHN SWINTON**, Professor in Practical Theology and
Pastoral Care, University of Aberdeen

"*Accompanying Disability* is a beautiful and honest collaborative
theological project between a theologian and his disabled father.
Accompaniment theology offers a new way of doing disability theology that honors first-person disability narratives and accompanying
theological reflections on caregiving."

—**DEVAN STAHL**, Associate Professor of Religion, Baylor University

"Intrepidly joining his father on his difficult journey from avid hiker
to quadriplegic, minister and theologian Topher Endress invites us
to think anew about accompaniment and disability theology *from the
perspective of the caregiver*. A powerful testimony to how to give care
and keep company with those in need."

—**BONNIE J. MILLER-MCLEMORE**, author of *Follow Your Bliss
and Other Lies about Calling* and E. Rhodes and
Leona B. Carpenter Chair and Professor Emerita of Religion,
Psychology, and Culture, Vanderbilt University

"Topher Endress offers a groundbreaking account of accompaniment theology in this moving and personal book. Never before have disability theologians so directly and sensitively addressed the plight of allies who care about and want to speak up for disabled people without speaking over them. This academically rigorous and eminently readable volume marks a new era in disability theology."

—**BRIAN BROCK**, Professor of Moral and
Practical Theology, University of Aberdeen

"Endress marvelously merges the role of pastor, theologian, and caregiver in this book that brings the reader into a better understanding of disabilities—not just the clinical understandings of disabling conditions, but more so in how we connect emotionally and relationally with and alongside individuals with disabilities."

—**CHRIS SNOW**, Pastor, North Hill Christian Church
(Disciples of Christ), Spokane, Washington

"Through the weaving of Endress's personal experiences and extensive study of topics related to disability, he invites the reader into the world of people affected by disability. The book includes stories told through the varied lenses of friend, son, student, teacher, ally, advocate, father, and caregiver. He introduces to disability theology an emphasis on the caregiver, those who accompany, the ones who are with the disabled. He writes about this challenging and transformative role that he terms accompaniment theology. I hope this will be a conversation that will be entered into with humility and curiosity as we imagine how Christ accompanies us."

—**PAM HARMON**, Church Consultant, With Ministries

"The stories of disabled people often do not fit the patterns of society, but the stories of those who accompany people with disabilities sometimes even do not fit disability discourses. In a personal voice and not eschewing the hard questions, Endress carves out the much-needed theological and pastoral space for a theology of accompaniment."

—**ARMAND LÉON VAN OMMEN**, Senior Lecturer in
Practical Theology, Codirector of the Center for
Autism and Theology, University of Aberdeen

"With an accessible, relatable tone and rich insights into the worlds of caregiving and disability, Endress tackles tricky topics of identity and interdependence with wisdom and grace. *Accompanying Disability*'s captivating father-and-son narrative demonstrates the manifold ways our stories intersect with and diverge from each other."

—**KEITH DOW**, Manager of Organizational and Spiritual Life, Karis Disability Services, and author of *Formed Together: Mystery, Narrative, and Virtue in Christian Caregiving*

"A profound gift to caregivers, this moving book explores the sacredness of shared journeys, weaving stories and theological insights to reveal how our lives can be transformed as we accompany our loved ones faithfully."

—**ERIK CARTER**, Luther Sweet Endowed Chair in Disabilities, Baylor University

"In *Accompanying Disability*, Endress presents a theology of lived experience in its fullest form. He weaves together deep theological reflection and personal narrative with a palpable sense of humanity. His writing strikes a rare and delicate balance of being both deeply thoughtful and wholly accessible, philosophical yet profoundly practical. In honoring his father's legacy, Endress has created something truly significant: a book that both informs and transforms. For theologians and for anyone who has faced—or will face—the realities of caregiving, this work will be an indispensable companion."

—**KATIE CROSS**, Christ's College Lecturer in Practical Theology, University of Aberdeen

"Endress's personal account is full of candor and wonder. His theological reflection draws the reader in and beautifully invites us to consider both the responsibility and the gift of accompaniment. This journey is well worth taking as Endress points us to the God who will always go with us."

—**PHIL LETIZIA**, author of *Held in the Love of God: Discipleship and Disability*

"It is a rare gift to realize the significance of a term in its first publication in the moment. Endress introduces the term *accompaniment theology* as a distinct branch of disability theology. This book will literally be the reference point for this topic for decades to come. His balance of respect and irreverence makes the topic accessible and engaging. It is emotional without being maudlin, informative without being arrogant, and holy without being sanctimonious. The interaction between father and son is powerful, reminding all readers that all roles shift over time. The reality of these changing roles creates space for learning to give care *and* receive care with dignity and grace."

—**AMY E. JACOBER**, author of *Redefining Perfect: The Interplay between Theology and Disability*

Accompanying Disability

Accompanying Disability
Caretaking, Family, and Faith

Topher Endress
with
John Endress

WESTMINSTER
JOHN KNOX PRESS
LOUISVILLE • KENTUCKY

© 2025 Topher Endress

First edition
Published by Westminster John Knox Press
Louisville, Kentucky

25 26 27 28 29 30 31 32 33 34—10 9 8 7 6 5 4 3 2 1

All rights reserved. No part of this book may be reproduced or transmitted in any form or by any means, electronic or mechanical, including photocopying, recording, or by any information storage or retrieval system, without permission in writing from the publisher. For information, address Westminster John Knox Press, 100 Witherspoon Street, Louisville, Kentucky 40202-1396. Or contact us online at www.wjkbooks.com.

Unless otherwise indicated, Scripture quotations are from the New American Standard Bible, Copyright © 1960, 1971, 1977, 1995, 2020 by The Lockman Foundation. Used by permission. All rights reserved. Scripture quotations marked NIV are from the Holy Bible, New International Version. Copyright © 1973, 1978, 1984, 2011 by Biblica, Inc.® Used by permission of Zondervan. All rights reserved worldwide.

Some names and identifying details have been changed to protect the privacy of individuals.

Book design by Drew Stevens
Cover design by Marc Whitaker / MTWdesign.net

Library of Congress Cataloging-in-Publication Data

Names: Endress, Topher, author. | Endress, John, author.
Title: Accompanying disability : caretaking, family, and faith / Topher
    Endress with John Endress.
Description: First edition. | Louisville ; Kentucky : Westminster John Knox
    Press, [2025] | Summary: "Through his personal narrative and Bible-based
    reflections, Topher Endress shows how the way we think about disability
    can have a profound impact on our ability not just to provide care or
    engage respectfully but to truly accompany loved ones with disabilities
    along our mutual journey of life"-- Provided by publisher.
Identifiers: LCCN 2025001920 (print) | LCCN 2025001921 (ebook) | ISBN
    9780664269166 (paperback) | ISBN 9781646984244 (ebook)
Subjects: LCSH: Endress, John. | Christian biography--United States. |
    Disabilities--Religious aspects--Christianity. | Human body--Religious
    aspects--Christianity. | Families--Religious aspects--Christianity. |
    LCGFT: Biographies.
Classification: LCC BR1725.E5194 E63 2025 (print) | LCC BR1725.E5194
    (ebook) | DDC 270.092 [B]--dc23/eng/20250215
LC record available at https://lccn.loc.gov/2025001920
LC ebook record available at https://lccn.loc.gov/2025001921

Most Westminster John Knox Press books are available at special quantity discounts when purchased in bulk by corporations, organizations, and special-interest groups. For more information, please e-mail SpecialSales@wjkbooks.com.

To Sam, my wife,
for giving me the space (and late nights)
to write this book.
And to John, my father,
for writing with me, in life and in death.

Contents

Introduction

Close your eyes and picture a disability. What do you see? Perhaps the symbol of accessibility, the near-ubiquitous white stick figure sitting in a wheelchair? Or maybe you are picturing a set of hearing aids, a crutch, or a ramp. Maybe you are seeing a person you know, with their specific disability highlighted.

Ask a group of people to picture "disabilities," and you will likely get back a different answer for every single person. Despite how concrete and material the experience often is, disabilities are a pretty tough concept to define. People with disabilities, even those with the same diagnoses or labels, are often so different and distinctive in how they experience the world that coming up with a solid definition that fits everyone's reality is an impossible task. And that isn't even considering the radically different types of disability; after all, what is it that knits together a man with cerebral palsy using a powered wheelchair and a woman with significant cognitive disabilities, or a veteran with post-traumatic stress disorder and a Deaf child?[1]

Sometimes categorizations of disability are legal. Sometimes they are medical. Schools make use of set criteria to decide who gets certain services, like extra time for tests or in-class notetakers. Disabled people are eligible for certain legal and economic aids but are restricted from many others. Drawing a line to say who is in and who is out is important in those cases. It is a very blurry line, in most instances. "What is a disability?" is an important, challenging question; the deeper question, though, is "Who gets to define a disability?"

Disabilities are inherently more complex than we ever tend to acknowledge, at least in public spaces. It's far easier to turn disabilities into the object of our pitying gazes, or the subject of our scientific research, and far harder to say with any credibility that there is pride to be had in disabilities alongside the pain. Naming a particular set of genes that produce a series of uncommon phenotypes takes scientific effort, but it is ultimately easy. Naming the ways we are irreversibly changed by the presence of disability, whether it is our own life or someone else's, is a much less straightforward task. But that's what I want to do. I want to explore how disabilities are normal and natural, yet shock our systems and break apart our expectations of the world. I want to see the pain and the reality of disabilities that hurt while holding space for disabilities that make the world more fun, more loving, more whole. I want to acknowledge that a disability is a *thing*, but it also shows the *absence* of a thing in our society. I want to ask these big questions and figure out what we do because of them.

In many cases, to be disabled is to be different—and worse off as a result. Fortunately, thanks to countless self-advocates and allies, there has been an emerging shift in this pattern of thinking. "Disability" is rapidly becoming a term that is less loaded with prejudice and more focused on naming what supports and accommodations someone may need to be fully part of their community. There is much more to be done, of course, but good things are happening.

Sadly, often these good things are happening in spite of the church, rather than because of it. Historically, the church has always been a pretty mixed bag when it comes to disabilities—sometimes doing wonderful work to support and care for people, sometimes doing really terrible things in the name of

God. Disabled people have been subject to ostracism, pity, and even torture at the hands of Christians, even as disabled people have found solace, love, and welcome at other times. Theology can be used for good or harm. Helpful theology is a blessing, leading to better care and a deeper relationship to faith. Bad theology, which connects disabilities and mental illness to a lack of faith, sin, or demons, is a curse many still live under.

Disability theology is the conceptual work being done to try to understand disability issues from multiple angles, seeking to be responsive to the lived experience of people while focusing on the "big picture" stuff like "What makes a person a person?" and "How is God active in the world?" Disability theology asks questions about God's providence, or what it means to find healing, or why things like genetic divergences exist. But beyond the big, philosophical stuff, the day-to-day experience of disability is no less important to theology. Disability theology is the work of trying to navigate the church's role in the world, God's action in the world, and human diversity, all while holding together these strands of specific personal experiences alongside historic philosophy and theology. It is, safe to say, a tough—and wonderful—field. Thinking theologically about disabilities offers us a way to engage real problems in the world and offer real answers. But that work is hard. How do you maintain a claim that there is an order to the world when a man becomes a quadriplegic? How do you look a parent in the eye and tell them you believe in a God who is good even when they find out their child has a disability that is likely to lead to an early death?

One of the main tenets of disability theology is that the people who actually experience disabilities ought to be the people most responsible for leading the conversations. That is not always the case, of course. For one, a lot of historic theology was written by nondisabled people, and it wouldn't be fair or wise to throw out thousands of years of their work. And second, disability is not located only in the lives of disabled persons themselves.

Those of us who care for disabled people in our lives have a different, but no less important, experience. We inhabit a particular role that is related to, but not identical to, the experience of being disabled. Disability theology helps us see the overlaps, and differences, in those experiences. There are of course disabled caregivers, too, but in this book, I am focused on a story of caregiving itself.

This book has several important functions, I hope. First, it widens who we imagine is capable of doing theology. One does not need to study theology at a world-class university, writing with constant reference to old dead men, to be a theologian. Theology is worked out among us as the people of God. There is certainly a role for the writings of old dead men to play, and much of it is quite good, even, but I hope you can find your own voice as a theologian with something to offer the world, formal degrees or not. Disability theology is helpful in naming that life experience is a form of theology, and it allows us all the freedom to see our own stories as powerful narratives that expose God's work in the world.

Second, this book advocates for a new division to emerge in this field: accompaniment theology. The field of disability theology is a small but important intersection that addresses the lived experience of some one billion humans across the globe. Often, the field is a churning sea of disabled voices, parents and caregivers, and interested folks who aren't totally sure why this burns as a passion within them. For a number of years, I fell into that last category—a minister who cared about students with disabilities. Then, suddenly, I transitioned overnight into the second, when my own father suffered a debilitating fall and became a quadriplegic.[2] Learning from disabled theologians, scholars, and faithful Christians has been integral to my own faith journey, and I hope to provide a shift in focus from lumping together anything to do with disability and instead offer a more nuanced division between the theological insights and experiences of disability and the insights and theology of accompaniment and caregiving.

Disability and accompanying disability are not the same experience, but the work each uncovers is universally useful to the church and to those whose lives are shaped by disability—theirs or a loved one's. To be disabled is to be in a particular set of relations with the world and the people around you, so naturally those who are on the other side of those relationships have a critical part to play. Acknowledging that these experiences are different, but intimately connected, allows all of us to learn from one another more richly and powerfully, exposing the ways that God is at work in our lives, in the lives of those around us, and in the wider world too. My hope is that by carving out clear space for those of us who experience caregiving, we can open even more space concurrently for disabled voices to have their own dedicated platform, making that much more clear the ways God is moving among us all in particular ways.

With more clarity about what life looks like for those who support, love, and care for disabled people, we can begin to see the theology that is written by so many different experiences. It might be easy to say that God is at work in a given situation, but it is much harder to say how without exploring the challenges and joys of being disabled. Likewise, when we divide out the experience of caregiving, naming it as a particular site where God is present, we can see the overlaps and differences more clearly. Caregivers and disabled people need one another, and need to know that their experiences are deeply worthwhile to the wider church.

In this vein, I believe sharing my father's story next to my own theological reflections opens a particular and important distinction in the field. If disabilities are rooted in experience, it does no favors to combine the firsthand experience of disabled people with the secondhand experience of those who care for them. The field of disability theology is growing and being reshaped as more and more people begin to see the importance of the work, which means more and more disabled voices are being taken as serious sites of theological generation. Rather than simply supplanting the nondisabled voices in the field, what we need is a new term, a new category that more accurately describes the work that God has set before us. I deem this "theologies of accompaniment."

Too often, being a caregiver means being focused on someone

else at the expense of being cared for yourself. Maybe you feel like your own story has been lost in favor of someone else's needs. Maybe you are feeling empty, not cared for in the ways you need and unable to give any more. I hope this book is in some sense a practical help for those who are struggling to provide adequate care to someone they love.

Caregiving is hard. It is often thankless. Regularly, people get burnt out and can't find anyone else to cover them, so they continue to work without breaks even to the detriment of those they serve. If that is you, I'm sorry that I can't offer you any material respite. I won't be showing up at your house to cook, clean, or do laundry while you take a nap. But maybe knowing another person's story, seeing what struggles and joys someone else has experienced, and knowing that you are not alone in navigating this world will be a small help to you. It is good to know that we are not alone.

This book is for any number of people. Pastors who want insight into lives that look different from their own, so they can provide better care. Disabled people who are interested in hearing how the people around them might be experiencing their role as caregivers. And most especially, accompanists themselves, looking to see their lives reflected in these pages.

God is at work in all of our stories and lives, no matter how burnt out or burdensome you feel.

1

Narrative

Telling a Story

I attend conferences on theology.

My dad attends conferences on land reclamation. Well, he did.

At the time when we—my father and I—began writing this book, I was a PhD student in between stints as a congregational minister. As a young, fledgling academic in a pre-COVID world, with a relatively small number of publications to my name, I was always keen to attend conference after conference. Partly, I needed to be rubbing as many elbows as I possibly could—jobs in academia don't exactly grow on trees, and it isn't lost on me that the number of folks self-categorizing as "religious," while still a vast majority of the planet, is shrinking. So any opportunity to network, whether it was in Dublin, Ireland, or Dublin, Ohio, always felt like an investment in my potential career. Every presentation was another line on the CV, which would hopefully one day impress someone enough to consider me for an interview.

I'm not sure it was ever really working. But, hey, most conferences come with free lunch, at least.

My dad, on the other hand, was at the very tail end of a long career. One day, on a visit home just after yet another conference on theology, I walked into his room and caught him on a call with some group, referred to by some long acronym whose true name I wouldn't even hazard a guess at. After, he mentioned he was unlikely to join any more of their meetings, as he thought he had nothing more to offer them in terms of expertise, acquired through years of driving the back roads of the state, traipsing through farms and wild hills, and making hand-drawn survey maps in an era just before Google Earth. Having spent a few decades as one of the very few credible voices able to speak across the aisle to two major institutions of our area—coal mining companies and the government—meant that he was a sought-after expert. Very rarely did he need to attend a conference just to pad a résumé; he may, however, have attended a few simply for the food.

Growing up, whenever I'd walk into his office, built into a corner of our basement, I'd find him on his computer poring over spreadsheets, at his light table making quick marks on massive maps of the countryside, or on the phone with some high-up at a local coal company, soliciting more work projects for his one-man consulting business. It would be common for my mom to have to yell down the enclosed staircase at least twice, often more, to remind him to come up and eat dinner with us. It wasn't familial negligence; it was what was necessary to keep things running. Certainly, he was there for our recitals, plays, tennis matches, homework help, and some general hangout time, but the price of being flexible enough to be involved in our lives was that "work time" became default. When he wasn't actively taking time off to do something, he was hard at work.

Postdisability, when I walked into his bedroom, a new space built on to the first floor to accommodate his physical needs after his accident, it was far more likely that he'd be lying around and listening to some Bob Dylan, or maybe Emmylou Harris or Todd Snider. Or, if it was between Halloween and January, he might be watching the movie *Bad Santa* for the umpteenth time. The rest of the family has no idea why he developed such a strong affinity for that movie in particular, but frankly a great deal about my dad defied explanation. Whether it was music or movies, his default time became something different. Finding him at work, then, was an odd sight, even if once familiar.

Writing about a person after they have died is a particular project. It is difficult, but considerably easier than writing about someone who is present. It gives you freedom to say what you want, since they can't really object. But that freedom begets honesty, and honesty makes writing all that much harder. This book was initially a project between the two of us—a caregiver with a background in disability theology and an actually disabled man. One at the beginning of a career, the other at the end. Only some of it was ever completed together, though. The more I wrote, particularly after his death, the bigger the challenge became: What if I wrote something he would have disagreed with? What if I wrote something too personal that he wouldn't have wanted shared? Who gets to decide those things, and what is right?

Everything is a question of ethics. Or at least, I think it is. But then, that's what I study: ethics, disabilities, and theology.

My dad's field, land reclamation, is the process of "resetting" the land (and soil and vegetation and animal life) after it's been used by humans. Primarily, he worked for coal companies, a common enough employer in southern Indiana in the 1980s and '90s, acting as the middleman between companies that wanted to spend as little money as possible and a series of often-contradictory government regulations that rarely considered feasibility or cost in their demands. He was of the opinion that lofty bureaucratic idealism was never going to lead to a healthy treatment of the land, just as unrestricted use without demand for restoration would lead to ruined environments. As such, he had a lot to say about the problems of a government that regulated issues beyond its understanding. It could be assumed, given that his work naturally served to hold coal companies' feet to the fire by enforcing said regulations, that he also said a great deal about corporate interests through his actions.

In fact, at one point in his life, he testified in a federal case against his own employer, causing them to spend millions on cleanup projects. However, in doing so, he exposed a series of regulations that made essentially no practical sense when it came to caring for the environment. From what I've heard, it was a point of pride for him, knowing that he refused to compromise his principles in order to assuage either side of the suit.

I like to think that I carry some of that principled pragmatism in me.

Much to the chagrin of my father, I vacillate between buzzing my hair into something appropriate for office work and growing it long like a Gen X slacker, temporally displaced but still clinging to my flannel, unkempt beard, and strange love of early 1990s alt-rock. It is likely that I'll be in my running shorts (the *short* running shorts, the kind that require a brief liner in order to not be obscene) and on my way out for a short seven-miler. I tend to let my hobbies dictate what I wear to the office, which means that I have absolutely written sermons in spandex and peer-edited journal articles dressed like Shannon Hoon. But hey, I have great legs, so I don't see the problem with the running gear, and Blind Melon was awesome, so I don't see a problem with the disaffected postrock look, either.

These are, of course, the things that I would say about myself.

If you had asked my dad about who he is, he'd likely have led with something about being a husband, a father, or a newly minted grandfather. He may have mentioned his love of the outdoors, especially the Great Smoky Mountains. He may have mentioned that he was born and raised in Evansville, Indiana, and that apart from his years attaining two degrees at Purdue University, he continued to live in his hometown for his entire life.

He likely would have skipped some of the other aspects, like being someone who impressively ran his own business during a volatile era for coal companies and being athletically competitive with himself to the point of injury many times throughout his life.

You would, assuming you had a conversation of any real length, determine for yourself that he was a kind and good-natured fellow, someone who would be polite to strangers as a baseline but could be quickly persuaded into quick-witted banter. You might pick up a sarcastic streak, although one that lacked the bite of someone who was actually rude. You'd certainly note a level of confidence and intelligence, though he would never be one to show off.

I don't know when in your conversation he would have mentioned the 500-pound elephant in the room. Or rather, the 500-pound wheelchair he used for mobility. Maybe it would have been acknowledged if he had needed to take a pressure break, mentioning that he was going to move his chair in a way rarely seen in public. Or, if he had a muscle spasm and needed to be repositioned in order to access his controls again. Maybe, if you were interacting closely, he'd have accidentally run over your toe when you weren't paying enough attention to his trajectory and your environment. He would apologize, of course, but if it was your own fault he wouldn't have felt too beat-up about it.

I watched him go from an energetic, surprisingly fit man of a certain age to a man who used an electric wheelchair, controlled by sensors placed in a half-halo around his head. Before his accident, he cycled. He played basketball. He hiked. He played tennis. He was the kind of dad who would learn whatever sports his children picked up, just so he could help us practice (and, I think, because he enjoyed being a good athlete and because he loved being a part of his children's lives, which should go without saying, but often can't).

The stories that follow are not a work of loss. This is a work of life. And as anyone tasked with caregiving knows, life includes loss. His life included loss before his accident, and it included loss after his accident. In some ways, his accident itself was a loss, though in other ways it wasn't.

Or perhaps that's what I want to be true. Maybe I want his life to be somehow unchanged across the chasm that was becoming a quadriplegic. I don't want his life to be marked by a disability. I know this seems like a devaluation of the entire concept, which seems odd given my commitment to people with disabilities. For whatever reason, making disability into something big, all-shaping, and totally changing one's life seems like a simple way to pit the disability against the life of the disabled person. That is something that seems quite easy to do in our society, fixating on something we deem a "problem" and ignoring the actual person behind the label we've thrown on top.

When I come home and my dad is working on this conference call, just like when, as a child, I used to run down the stairs and across the concrete floor and into the closet where we had a spare refrigerator to grab some sugar-laden syrupy soft drink and I'd see him across the open unfinished basement, staring into his maps, I see a man who lives consistently over time. And when I come home to see him lying in his specialty hospital bed, I see a man who has changed far beyond the expected order. How do I understand this man, my father? How does it work to be a minister and a son, or a theologian in the house of the people who taught you to use a toilet, or a disability scholar pushing the chair of a disabled man who is at once so much more and never less? How can I know who he was, and is, and will be, and therefore who I am?

I may never know. But if I shine a light on different aspects of our shared lives together, if I shine light onto our *time*, our *economy*, our *history*, our *spaces*, our *performances*, maybe I'll find something true about John Endress. Something that is true about the work God calls us into. Something true about what it means to accompany.

Accompaniment cannot be distilled to these five themes, but through them we can see something begin to take shape. Namely, that whatever lens we use to explain our life, and the life of those we care for, there is a Spirit moving within it, knitting together these different perspectives into one cohesive life. Each person's story is complex, of course, but more importantly it is sacred. That means that trying to explain someone's life is an act of describing our own theology; there is something at stake in trying to determine a theology of accompaniment, a theology contextualized by caregiving and navigating the overlaps and boundaries of disparate lives which are bound together— the authenticity of the claims we make about God.

FINDING AN ABLED PLACE
IN DISABLED SPACES

At disability conferences, the most common question is "What brings you here?" That really means "Which acceptable narrative describes you?" It has become the price of entry into these communities; give us your story, justify your presence here, and we will accept you as "belonging." There is often a real sense of distrust from the outset, primarily because so much of the world is openly hostile to folks with disabilities. Eugenics is alive and well in our world, but that's a discussion for later. Most people, and families, with disabilities have endured countless acts of aggression, from needing to prove one's haplessness in order to receive aid such as Individualized Education Programs (IEPs) or veterans' benefits to being openly excluded from civil or human rights like marriage, housing, or earning a living wage. In such an ableist world, most people simply can't be trusted, so in order to participate in disability conferences, they need to be able to prove their own credentials. Us able-bodied people, particularly white men, have yet to prove that we are regularly worthy of that trust, so in order to be accepted we must give something up, we must locate ourselves in the wider narrative in some public fashion, typically around the first coffee break.

The acceptable narratives are limited in scope, but shift depending on context. There's the very common "parent of a child with disabilities." When I walk around, most people probably assume I have a child or maybe a sibling with some sort of significant disability. Maybe they assume I have a parent who has some sort of degenerative disability like Alzheimer's or dementia, but as a man I'm way less likely to be encouraged or mandated to become their caregiver, so I doubt that's an assumption any make.

As a caregiver, you have a narrative. Sometimes, it is a lot less "standard" than what other people want it to be. It is easier to understand someone if you can put them into a box, but caregiving is too wide, diverse, and complex for that to be truly helpful. You might be caring for a child with significant intellectual delays, an adult child with addiction struggles, an aging parent, a spouse who has had an accident, or any number of situations; even if the general story can be told, it doesn't mean people will actually grasp what your life looks like. It is OK to be frustrated by people who think they can understand your life based on a single story, trope, or label.

In theological contexts, another common narrative is "religious leader just now realizing disabilities are, like, a *thing*." Our religious training institutions have long shied away from teaching about disabilities in any meaningful way, and while that's a fairly bold and far-reaching attack, I stand by it because our religious institutions have been very up-front about their own oversights in this field. It is incredibly common to talk with a minister who can't name more than three people with disabilities in their congregation. Bear in mind, the national average is over one in every four people, so any congregation with more than a dozen or so worshipers likely contains more than three disabled people.[1] Ministers, chaplains, and other religious leaders have no more proven themselves faithfully safe than the politicians who make life miserable for disabled folk, especially when one considers the damage of theologies that prioritize faith healings or link ill health to lack of belief or outright sin. I regularly meet ministers who boldly proclaim that "we don't have any disabled people here" as if it was some sort of valid excuse for ignoring support needs, rather than a condemnation of how oblivious they themselves are as people.

All too rare in many "disabled spaces" are, surprisingly, actual people with a disability / disabled people. I name both terms because labels are political, and these seemingly similar titles are used in very different ways. "Person with a disability," which uses "person first" language, names that the person in question is just that—a person. The disability doesn't define them, it's just one aspect of who they are. In some sense, that's helpful because it reminds us that disabled people are also doctors and professors and janitors and bowling alley enthusiasts and accordion players and fans of *Parks and Rec* and hopeful and fearful and happy and sad and all the other things that make up being a person. Conversely, "disabled person" reminds us that to erase the disability is to erase the person. You can't be *you* if you stop "having" autism. The child with Down syndrome would be a completely different child without that third copy of their twenty-first chromosome, just as I wouldn't be *me* if I weren't white, straight, or male. "Disabled person" challenges us to not see disability as something inherently negative or something to be purposefully ignored.

I don't fit neatly into these accepted categories of disability conference attendee. My story began in earnest when I was a university student serving as a youth group leader for high school students. As a young guy, eager to invite others into the world of faith I had rediscovered during my own high school days, I was quick to say yes to pretty much anything that would welcome more kids into our community. I was happy to be the awkwardly old guy chatting with loner kids sitting on the fringes of the student section of high school basketball games, even as I was front and center of our university student section on other nights (often noticeable on TV due to my bright gold spray-painted jorts and pink hair). I was happy to meet students for lunch, sitting on the floor against lockers, even as my classmates were taking afternoon naps in the quad on sunny days (or, far more common in northern Indiana, napping on the student union couches on cold, windy days). I wanted these kids to experience the revelations I had, so when a student decided he wanted not only to come along to our weekly gatherings but also to join us for our weeklong summer camps, I was quick to welcome him in.

I did not suspect that the student, whom I will call Barry, would pose much of a challenge to integrate with the group, although he had some support needs of which I was frankly ignorant. Barry has several diagnoses of various disabilities, each one intersecting with the others in ways that only made sense in his own body and in his own experience; another student with the same named disabilities would have been entirely different. When I needed help guiding Barry through our group discussions, or when I wasn't sure how to help Barry engage with other students, my efforts to find appropriate supports fell on similarly ignorant ears. The adults in my life, particularly those in charge of the overall ministry I worked with, those whom I trusted to help me navigate the world of disability support, knew only platitudes and general advice. Only two, a couple who were willing to welcome Barry into their own lives, to learn about him *from* him, were able to help. For their witness and example, I am continually grateful.

But as for the majority of ministry guides and theological texts? Mostly bullshit. That's why I started to really dig in and study disability theology. That's when it became obvious that God "placed disabilities on my heart," which is a phrase I say when I'm speaking to Baptists. The disappointment in the available literature led me to seminary, and eventually to my PhD focus.

But this long story doesn't really work when meeting people at disability conferences. It doesn't fit any of the accepted narratives. Still, it's what I claim, even if it takes more explanation than just saying, "My dad is disabled."

Your story might not be very straightforward either. Being a caregiver can look radically different, person to person, and that isn't always easily seen or accepted. You might not even call yourself a caregiver right now, even if you provide love, support, and regular care for someone. That's OK, too. You know the facts of your own life better than anyone, label or not. Like the term "disability," "caregiver" is also blurry. There are some specific legal definitions, of course, that impact taxes and particular rights, but I want to suggest that plenty of caregivers operate well outside of those boundaries. What we need, therefore, is a better language for what God is doing in our lives, a theology of caregiving that can support us, guide us, and challenge us.

WHO OWNS A STORY?

The conference was originally supposed to be held in Durham, North Carolina. Sadly, upon viewing the grounds of Duke Divinity School, it was determined that the Summer Institute on Theology and Disability could not be hosted on such an inaccessible campus. While the school was open to hosting, including making available campus rooms for attendees, it just didn't seem reasonable to ask participants who required mobility support to endure a constant stream of unfriendly architecture and design all week. Rather than being on Duke's campus, with its beautiful English Gothic stone facades and impressive chapel, we were relocated to downtown Raleigh.

I have nothing against Raleigh; it was a nice place to visit and a lovely little city. But a downtown setting for an international conference offers some challenges in terms of accessibility, too. Namely, it was expensive as hell and a lot of the sidewalks were in a sad state, given the amount of use they got each day.

As a student, or more accurately, as a young person who was poor enough to be pitied by the conference director yet dependable enough to have shown up to volunteer at this same conference several times, I was tasked on the first day with stuffing info sheets into folders and handing out name badges. The institute draws a reasonable amount of new faces each year. Still, there are only so many people working in the intersection of theology and disabilities, so a good chunk of us insist on coming along annually. It is a place where people just *get it*, and you don't have to explain the absolute basics to someone who has never once considered "disability" as a meaningful category. That shared language allows conversations to settle in quickly, where there is some implicit trust that the person you are talking with has already learned to more or less straddle the ever-shifting line between acknowledging disabilities and not fixating on them.

As the registration period died down and attendees made their way to hotels or happy hours, Bill, the director, came over to where I was fitting unused folders back into storage boxes to introduce a lone straggler—a middle-aged, though youthful, man called Shane. He was an Australian theologian who flew to North Carolina from across the world just to offer a keynote on his recent book. His tousled blond hair and casual demeanor immediately brought the words "surfer dude" to my mind, although the motorized wheelchair likely meant that surfing wasn't the most accessible activity for him.

Bill thought I might help this jet-lagged theologian navigate the city in advance of that evening's program. When most people went to rooms to change, nap, or grab a quick bite, Shane knew he was probably better off exploring the area and looking for barrier-free paths between the buildings we'd be using that week. Fair enough. I've seen enough massive gaps in sidewalks and poorly signaled construction projects that even I, as a very mobile man, can grasp how challenging it must be to get around in many cities.

We decided to try our luck and headed the four blocks to the church where we had been invited for an optional evening prayer before the conference's opening session. As we began making our way through the strangely doughnut-shaped lobby of the hotel, Shane zipped ahead of me, as if my own feet were some sort of disability that he in his chair had overcome. Noticing quickly that I, unaccustomed to someone using a wheelchair moving so much more quickly than my father, was effectively left in his dust, Shane paused and turned back with a quizzical gleam in his deep-set eyes.

"Sorry," I answered, perhaps overeager to avoid any social faux pas in front of a major professor at the start of an important conference. "I'm not used to chairs being driven that fast!"

He cocked his head slightly and asked the obvious follow-up: "Oh, do you work with quads?" Meaning: Why would you be familiar at all with wheelchairs? How did you earn your place at the disability table?

NEWS REPORT: JOHN

Hiker Evacuated after Smoky Mountain Fall

GATLINBURG, Tenn. (Oct. 10, 2010)— An Indiana man who was injured while hiking on a remote trail in Great Smoky Mountains National Park on Sunday afternoon was rescued by a team from the park.

Park Ranger Brad Griest was responding to a call about a distressed hiker when he was told about the badly injured hiker farther up the Alum Cave Trail. The second hiker, identified as John Endress, 55, had reportedly fallen and suffered possible head or spinal injury.

Hiking to where the man had fallen took Griest about 45 minutes.

The man said that he could not feel his body below his neck. Griest supported him with a cervical collar, gave him oxygen, and then monitored his vital signs until a 13-person litter crew arrived. The man was then strapped to a rigid backboard atop the litter and evacuated down the Alum Cave Trail. The crew had to maneuver the litter on steep ground, cross several creeks, and use rope belays. The injured hiker was accompanied by his son, who assisted in the evacuation.

The litter team reached the trailhead at 10 p.m., where they were met by a Gatlinburg Fire Department ambulance. Endress was taken to Sugarlands Visitor Center and then flown by Lifestar helicopter to the University of Tennessee Medical Center at Knoxville, the Level 1 trauma center closest to the park.

I was the hiker who informed Brad of the man who had fallen, after my first-ever trail run.

After my dad fell and I heard a deep, strange groan like I had never heard before, I knew something was wrong. We had been moving at a good clip, maybe 3.5 mph going downhill, our left sides against a glistening rock wall and our right sides open to the tops of trees growing on the steep mountainside. His foot hit a rock, or a root, or something, and he fell. His hands went out to brace himself, but fell impotent against the wet rock, the slick face offering no friction as he hit the ground at full force. I think there was another root where his neck landed; I really can't be sure.

I made sure, several times, in fact, to command him not to move his head (although he had already rolled onto his back nearly instantly). It was deeply ingrained in me that when someone falls, you don't let them move their head or neck. I'm not actually sure where that was instilled in me to begin with, to be honest. But it was the very first thing I thought of.

We were at a bend with a great view, maybe two miles up from a fairly popular trailhead. We had been hiking all day. We covered about twenty miles before the accident, and that meant at one point we were probably deep into a mountain trail some seven or eight miles from the nearest frequented spot. Even if we had run into someone else back where we had come from, what would they have done? But we weren't in those remote spots anymore. We were in a section of nature that by sheer luck had become a common tourist location. And that meant people.

Not many. Just one family, in fact. Two parents, a child. Young. Maybe eight? I was always bad with ages. Unfortunately, this was a family visiting Tennessee from Japan, and they spoke limited English. The little girl came up to us and offered a Band-Aid. Very sweet.

I was able to communicate reasonably effectively that under no circumstance should his head be moved, and then I left. I left my father, who had fallen and seemed to have done serious damage to himself, possibly a brain injury or who knows what, lying in the woods on the side of a mountain with a Japanese tourist family to keep him safe. And I ran.

I had never really run in the woods before. I didn't do cross-country in high school. I did tennis, and our running was usually sprints, nothing longer than a mile (and that was only when we were in trouble for goofing off). I really started running more in college. I tried to become a runner in high school, but it just didn't stick. My tennis coach gave me a running logbook as a senior gift, though, because she noticed that I seemed to earnestly try to break into the habit. And that book stuck. I kept it for years, through several moves, well after I switched all my running data to the panoptic apps that track my heart rate and cadence and VO$_2$ max.

As I raced down that mountain, I had two thoughts: "Do not fall, you are not helping him if you get hurt too. Mom would kill you if you died trying to get help for Dad," and "I'll have to look this route up later to put it in that book."

I don't always like the way my mind works.

For a long time, I would periodically google "when are you a real runner" as if some magic formula would tell me how many miles to run a week, how fast I needed to be, or how much my shoes would need to cost in order to credibly say, "I'm a runner." It felt like after years of trying to be something I knew I wasn't, I was really just acting. I'm not a real runner, I am just some weird tennis player who is doing cardio.

The first time I felt like a runner, I was on the final hour of an all-nighter of college. In my first year, on a crisp but reasonable October night, I sat in a twenty-four-hour computer lab drinking Monster Energy and eating Cap'n Crunch, filling in my biology lab notebook with all the missing data that I had collected but never adequately recorded. At 5:30 a.m., I finished. I didn't want to risk sleeping past the deadline at 8, so I went to my dorm, tried to change silently to not wake my roommate, and went for a run.

At night, after the bars have closed and the silence of rural Indiana finally falls on campus, there is a sense of peace and calm. School is all about doing doing doing, achieving and researching and growing and never standing still. But not at 5:45 in the morning.

By the time I turned the corner from Northwestern to State Street, students were lining up for the bars, eager to parlay their pregaming of OJ and vodka into Purdue's famed Breakfast Club, in which students dress in Halloween costumes and hit the bars on game days starting at 7 a.m. It's raucous, but fun. Very college. But before the laughter and shouts of the crowds, as I rounded the back side of the intramural fields and watched the sun come up, I felt like a runner. I felt powerful. Connected to the ground, feeling all the intricacies of the path as it wove side to side and up and down, an undulating river that beckoned me to explore it. There was peace. And promise. And challenge.

For the first time in my life, I was a runner.

The second time I felt that feeling, I was barreling down the trail past Alum Cave and Inspiration Point, wearing hiking boots and frantically checking for a phone signal. Every root, every rock, every blind bend, I felt it all and noticed it, even anticipated the bumps and cracks, because I couldn't afford to trip and fall like my dad had.

Claiming that Brad reached him forty-five minutes later, as per the news report, is a bit of a stretch. First, it took me about ten minutes to convince him that he should abandon his other distress call. Someone on the same trail, apparently, had fallen ill, and two emergency mountain rescue responders were headed to help. But I happened to catch Brad as they were loading up in the parking lot. Had I been slower, they might have gone up past me, down a fork that I missed, out of sight and unknown, never to make it to my dad. But I made it there as they were adjusting their packs, the trunk of their SUV still open.

"How did you know we needed you? Did someone manage to get a signal and call for help?"

"Yeah, we got a call about someone falling ill; they think it's a diabetic issue."

"What are you talking about? There's a man who had a fall on the trail and has possible head and neck injuries!"

"No, we have a call about someone falling ill."

"And I'm telling you, one of you is going to come with me instead."

Brad was wonderful. But at multiple points I did offer to carry his pack for him, as I thought it would speed us along. He generally kept about a 2 mph pace. In his defense, he needed to conserve energy, plus he was carrying an extra fifty pounds of gear. In spite of what I wanted at that moment, which was to charge up the mountain as fast as possible, he was well aware that the approach that offered the best chance at survival was one that was slow, methodical, and conservative. And in my defense, I knew I had left my injured father on the side of a mountain with little to no supervision, so I don't think my desire to rush was too unjustified.

NEWS REPORT: SHANE

Man Airlifted after Skate Ramp Fall

NOWRA, New South Wales (Oct. 10, 2010)—A local father of three was seriously injured Sunday in an accident at his church's skate ramp.

Shane Clifton, 39, was playing with his children when he dived off a bike into a pit filled with soft foam. He landed awkwardly on his head, neck, or back, according to his brother, Kurt Clifton, who witnessed the accident.

Paramedics arrived within minutes, and a helicopter flew the injured man to Prince of Wales Hospital, which has a dedicated spinal unit.

Shane Clifton, a Bible college professor and an avid surfer, has three children, ages 10, 13, and 15.

The skate ramp has been used often in the short time since it was installed at Nowra City Church, according to Pastor Peter Pilt. He said the church had "rigorous safety procedures" for the ramp and pit, calling this "an absolute lousy accident."

The congregation is "certainly believing and praying that he'll make a full recovery," Pilt said, although they are aware that these kinds of injuries can be life-altering. A break in the fifth vertebra, as he reportedly suffered, can lead to paralysis and further medical complications.

Kurt Clifton said that the family is in a state of shock. "Everyone can't believe that from what he did, he hurt himself in that way."

"Everyone can't believe that from what he did, he hurt himself in that way."

The same can be said for my dad, too. In fact, a number of people who came to visit him in the intensive care unit in Tennessee managed to make the macabre joke, all independently of one another. "Wow, for all the times John hurt himself doing something stupid, who would have guessed a simple fall on a hike would be what got him?"

I wouldn't say my dad was particularly accident-prone, but when he did injure himself it was always spectacular. One rainy afternoon, he decided to take a long bike ride, only to come back with half his elbow misplaced. I remember him coming in from his ride, bloodied and torn up. He walked in, showed my mom how the cap to his elbow was lodged halfway up his triceps, and asked, "Do you think I should see someone about this?" A year later, he broke the same elbow again, this time doing tricks on a trampoline.

Shane and my dad certainly shared a penchant for adventurous behavior, and ultimately both became quadriplegics through seemingly minor incidents (on the same day, no less), but their experiences are nonetheless unique. Losing certain physical abilities does not negate a person's right to be master of their own story, does it?

I became acutely aware of the challenge of deciding who has the right to tell certain stories, given that caregivers and care receivers are bound together but in vastly different roles, when later in that same conference Shane shared my—and my father's—story in his keynote speech. He pointed at me and used my father's name to make his point. I had been publicly outed. He did not ask me for permission, nor would I have felt myself capable of giving it. The jolt I felt when he spoke about my father to my colleagues, when I had been so guarded previously, told me that there was something important and challenging about this issue. It felt like a betrayal, a breach, and a violation of something that I personally held.

In fairness to Shane, I did not tell him *not* to share our conversation. We spoke at length about his accident, and my dad's, given the unbelievable coincidence of it all. His kids are roughly my age, so I assumed he was mining me for insight into how they might be processing their new roles. Plus, it is wild to think that their accidents occurred within twenty-four hours of each other and involved similar injuries. Perhaps, given their similar lifestyles, social roles, histories, and now injuries, Shane and my dad understood each other better than nearly anyone else on earth could. Maybe that gave Shane some right to talk about my dad's story, since it so matches his own.

But again, stories are sacred and point back to God. How we use stories is important, and if we take someone else's journey and use it to prove our own points, we are highlighting our own deficient understanding of God.

Is it OK, then, that I put Shane's shockingly similar story next to my dad's in this book? What if Shane personally shared his story with me, as I did with him? Is it OK because he has shared his story publicly, from a stage, and is the care receiver, rather than caregiver? When I did reach out to ask for his consent to share his story, Shane noted the same critical difference—that he shares his story publicly already—and therefore he had no reason to ask me not to share. In addition to his consent, he also offered a heartfelt apology, and he has done incredible work to accompany the LGBTQ+ community in Australia even at the expense of his theological career, lest anyone think that Shane is some villain, rather than a fellow person with a sacred story and rich, complex life.

It is important that we consider these questions of *who* owns what. It's not OK that white people get to take parts of another culture, decontextualize it and remove it from the broader context of minority life, and then earn money off it while boxing out the originators of those cultures. That idea is broadly accepted, now, and we generally seem to get that cultural appropriation is wrong, even if people might disagree on the exact boundaries between appropriation and respect.

But what is the right way to talk about your own life when it cannot be discussed without revealing the life of someone else? If you are a caregiver, your life is transformed by the presence of the person who relies on your care. How do we be respectful of someone else's story when it is part of our own? What do we owe to one another as the carriers of each other's stories?

Caregiving is messy work. Partly, because it usually involves things like cleaning up bodily fluids and dealing with confusing paperwork, financial strain, or challenging behaviors. If it is short-term, like doing all the driving because your husband broke his elbow, again, it is probably easy to see that this is just a blip within the big picture. But when the caregiver's work stretches on with no end in sight, the care recipient's needs lasting until death, the lines between our stories also get messy. Instead of just taking on some extra work until someone else's cast comes off, you have become something new and your whole life has shifted even though it is *their* body and *their* needs that you are responding to.

Here is where the terminology of "accompaniment" becomes critical. Nowhere in Scripture does God ask us to live lives that are utterly independent of one another. This is a point often highlighted by the disability community, particularly in theological spaces. With apologies to Paul Simon, no one is an island. Not only do we rely on vast networks of help for everything in our lives (Who is providing your electricity? Who is growing your food? Who made your clothes?), but we simply would cease to *be who we are* without the impact of those around us.

This is sometimes used as a neoliberal basis for something called "allyship." To act as an ally, one must desire a world in which people are treated equally, and then work toward that within the broken contexts in which we find ourselves. It requires that we partner with folks on the margins, using our relative powers and privileges to restructure spaces formerly unwelcoming into spaces that are open. I don't disparage the work of allyship; it is important and often holy work. Bringing a deeper engagement with God's justice into the world is never a bad thing! But to be an ally is to be focused on changing the environment. To accompany is to be changed, fundamentally, yourself.

To accompany is to participate in the Spirit in a process of becoming something you were not, and that shift functions to give this work a thoroughly theological focus. As theologian Roberto Goizueta argues, when we begin to see ourselves as bound to the stories of those around us, we will find that the work of God is enacted on the outskirts, the wild and untamed meeting places of everyday life, reshaping us through God's presence in even the most mundane of daily activities when shared.[2]

First Corinthians 12 offers us a deep look at what it means to accompany one another as Christians:

> For just as the body is one and *yet* has many parts, and all the parts of the body, though they are many, are one body, so also is Christ. For by one Spirit we were all baptized into one body, whether Jews or Greeks, whether slaves or free, and we were all made to drink of one Spirit.
> For the body is not one part, but many. (vv. 12–14)

There is tension, the unity of a single body and the diversity of many parts. Each has its own role, but the body cannot be described by any one or group of them. Indeed, the body is something necessarily composed of diverse differences, yet it also becomes more than the sum of these parts.

Theologian Brian Brock notes that Paul's language here concerning the body is fundamentally linked to *communication*. That is, how the body interacts with itself and all its diverse parts identifies the purpose of our bodies, individual and collective: to share stories and communicate that we are not simply individual actors working to make the world better, but that we only *exist* in this unified and diverse body.[3] It is the difference between taking action because you think it is the right thing to *do* and taking action because it is part of who you *are*.

I am, like many, one whose life has been irrevocably changed by the presence of a disabled person, or several, rather, and thus it is wholly appropriate to acknowledge that as one who seeks to accompany in a way that reflects God's movement in the world, I am capable of sharing such accompaniment theology in this book. It is who I *am*, built into my body because I am knit into the body of Christ in a particular way, dependent on the people whom I have accompanied throughout my life.

It is tautologically true that one cannot accompany alone. There must be some experience, tied to some other person, that serves as the groundwork for this type of reflection. That experience is only partly mine to tell. I have accompanied multiple people, but primarily my disabled father; as such, John himself will have to offer some of the work here.

In a powerful way that impacts not just theology but also politics, the increase in desire for firsthand narratives on disability drives a shift toward a deeper engagement with the actual needs, concerns, perspectives, and hopes of disabled people. The field of autism has seen a drastic shift from the stories of those caring for autistic children to the stories of autistic people told by themselves. Books like *The Reason I Jump*[4] and documentaries like *This Is Not about Me*[5] are products of modernity; they were written by nonspeaking autistic people using specialized communication technologies. In a bygone era, we would not have learned the inner thoughts of people who need alternative supports to communicate. Thanks to technology and awareness, partly driven by a desire to make the inner world known to outsiders, they have told their stories in ways that have shaped our understanding of autism for a new generation. Communication pads, Makaton, text-to-voice, voice-to-text, and all sorts of technological advancements have led to a world that is far more inclusive of the diverse experience of humanity. Their stories highlight how caregivers can also change with the times; sometimes, being a great caregiver means becoming a great advocate in educational spaces, learning new technologies, or helping carve out new spaces for the stories of care recipients to be shared.

In a similar way, but for different reasons, my father was able to write what he had written—what appears following each chapter of this book—only because a path was opened by technology. Yes, he still spoke audibly and could be readily understood after his accident. But there is something radical about typing away on your own terms, hidden in the safe sanctuary of a bedroom, and only inviting certain eyes to read the product when you've decided it should be read. For centuries, the idea of privacy has been laughable. Humans lived in close proximity, often with little more than curtains or thin walls to separate them. The rich relied heavily on servants, slaves, and various household help as well, so even they could not buy their privacy. The world was interconnected in a way that couldn't be hidden. Now in the wake of the "work from home revolution" post-COVID, the impending promise of driverless ride shares and drones delivering our groceries and packages (and fighting our wars), we can pretend we are isolated kings reigning over our delivery-subscription-filled realms. Other people are a choice, and we can control when and how we see them. But the reality is of course a far cry from this illusion.

No one is more acutely aware of the innate interdependence of life than disabled people. Someone to fix your wheelchair when it breaks, someone to scoot you onto your hoist to get you out of bed, someone to feed you, someone to deem you "disabled enough" to receive benefits, and so on. And too often, especially for those with autism and/or developmental disabilities, it has meant requiring someone else to share your story for you.

There is a tension, then, between acknowledging interdependence and seeking agency. My dad wrote his own stories, but I'm sharing them. The words are his, but the technology that allowed him to write them down was created many years prior. Accompaniment lives in this tension, as well. When we truly journey with someone, we play into a role that seeks to simultaneously lift up the agency and value of an individual while also practicing interconnectedness.

Accompaniment can be described through a number of lenses, but it cannot be reduced to them. It is a movement done in tandem with the Spirit and the others around you. It is like a birthday party. You cannot have a party alone; it requires other people. It has a shape, a context, and particularities that mark it as a specific event. There is a cultural shape to a birthday party, but one that changes based on age and social location. A twenty-first birthday in America is different from a sixth birthday. A fifteenth birthday for a Hispanic woman is different from a fifteenth birthday for an Asian woman. There are still shared overlaps, though the presence of particularities like balloons or cards does not turn a random gathering into a birthday party. Accompaniment is much the same; there are ways to dissect its meaning, but it is more than the sum of these parts.

In the coming chapters, I will attempt to draw a line through these lenses, looking deeply into how disability and life are expressed through time, economy, history, space, and performance, so that we might have a better, deeper, and more theologically oriented language for the ways that the lives of caregivers are fundamentally shaped and changed. This is the groundwork for accompaniment theology, written into the narrative for a father, a son, an accident, and everything in between.

Mountain Mysteries

It is curious how seemingly innocuous events when we are young have an indelible effect on us as we age. For myself, everyday activities greatly inspired a growing love of nature, especially areas that hosted tortuous terrain. As is true with most children born in my era, the 1950s, fun resulted from using our imagination and the natural resources of the neighborhood.

I spent hours exploring the land and woods adjacent to our house. My childhood home stood atop a hill—not a mountain, but a nice steep hill. When I was very young, my dad built a wood and tar paper shack in these woods just outside the boundary of our yard. A favorite picture shows my siblings and me dressed as pirates standing on top of the lean-to.

Behind our house sat some empty land that we called "the gullies." While many of the neighborhood kids would play back there periodically, I spent an unusual amount of time in the woods of the gully. Of course, it wasn't long before neighborhood development began. My friend Kim and I would gather all of the empty paint cans and leftover lumber we could find from the new home construction sites. We eventually took our stash and built bridges over the gullies using the paint cans as the foundation posts and the lumber as the walking bridge.

Whenever a new home was built in this growing neighborhood, large piles of dirt would appear as the land was prepared for construction. I would spend time playing on the dirt and eventually began to examine the dirt, trying to understand it. While I didn't know the technical terms at the time, I later discovered that I held a particular fascination with soil structure and how it could be separated by particle size. This was the start of my interest in soil and led me to study earth science and receive two degrees in the field.

During most of my career I worked for coal mining companies in southwest Indiana. Because I was drawn to the mountains, I felt especially fortunate when my work took me to eastern Kentucky and West Virginia. It occurred to me, over the course of time, that mining the land of southwest Indiana made it amazingly similar to that of the eastern Appalachians. Perhaps this similarity between the mined region of southwest Indiana and the eastern foothills leading to those mountains is what drew me to my career in land reclamation.

My childhood exploration and observation of the world around me set the stage for a wonderful career and an appreciation for nature. One particular family trip, however, was most memorable in the effect it had on my future.

When I was about twelve years old my family—mom, dad, four boys and one girl—took a trip to Niagara Falls. Niagara Falls was impressive, of course, but the indelible impression I took from the trip occurred earlier when we drove through the Appalachian Mountains near Wheeling, West Virginia. Despite my prior exposure to various types of land, there was something haunting about the Appalachians that never left me. This predilection eventually led to some of my life's most memorable moments—both good and bad.

2
Time

Recalculating Expectations

Although I was not the one doing the lion's share of the care-giving, when I was home for any length of time throughout college, grad school, my first job, and during my doctorate, I often helped with my father's transportation. We had a tan van with black trim and a Purdue plate in front, custom-fit to his wheelchair. It was a behemoth of a vehicle, taller than standard to account for a chair, and lower to the ground to make the extendable ramp useful. The middle row and the front passenger seat were pulled out, allowing him to navigate and spin while inside. The driver's seat was left mostly untouched, but the back bench was set high enough off the floor that they installed a footrest so folks could support their legs, rather than let them dangle like little kids' legs from a high chair.

Accessible vans aren't cheap. Most are easily in the $100,000 ballpark. But without one, especially given how most Americans are spread out, there would be little to no chance of participation in most aspects of life. For my father, who had a very significant disability but also a desire to participate in life, a van was a lifeline to the person he had been, wanted to be, and wanted to become. He wanted to keep going to church. He wanted to be able to visit his brother's house and go to holiday parties. He wanted to enjoy the fruits of a long life of hard work: seeing family and friends, serving and leading in the community, seeing his children become adults and move out.

My parents had roughly two and a half years of being "empty nesters" before his accident. They had expected to travel, to take the odd weekend trip here and there, to go to the weddings of their nieces and nephews and their friends' kids, to enjoy some peace and quiet. It isn't a phase of life that everyone gets, but it is one they worked toward. I imagine they held together the same mix of emotion that many adults hold when they see their final child move out of the house: pride, sadness, grief, love, excitement, hope, loss.

But after a short while of being an empty nester, my dad fell and became a quadriplegic who traveled back in time to a world where he was dependent on a routine and a space and a caregiver, much like a very young baby.

I say this not to infantilize him. He was not a child. But he was no longer an empty nester, either. He was a third thing, an adult with the needs of an adult *and* the needs of a child.

In her foundational essay on "crip time," Ellen Samuels highlights how disabled people relate to time in different ways than their nondisabled counterparts.[1] In some ways, crip time is just the acknowledgment that the world is not built with disability or accessibility in mind, and therefore plenty of disabled people find themselves without enough time to get to everything in a day.

Sometimes, being disabled makes some movements slower. A nondisabled person might leave their house, stop for coffee, and make it to work on time. A disabled person might be fifteen minutes late for doing the same.

And sure, when I was trying to help get my dad from the house to church, or even just from the van into a building, the process would take longer. And often, we *were* late to things.

First, getting him from the bed to his chair often took significant time. Typically, he'd need to be adjusted: his back angled just enough, but not too much; his shoulders slightly uneven, just enough to give his head the necessary range of motion to reach the controls; his chest, arms, hands, waist, and feet strapped in. We couldn't just pop into a convenience store, at least not without a huge process of unloading and reloading the chair into the van, so I'd have to be diligent in checking his bag for a wallet, extra jacket, meds, portable urinal, and the various other accessories that made his travel possible. I'd have to make sure his Foley catheter bag was empty before leaving, as well, because it's rude to empty it on a street and I might not find an accessible toilet. Then, back the van out of the garage and into the driveway, where there was sufficient space to maneuver, and make sure the heat was on no matter the time of year, since one of the physical losses from his accident was the ability to regulate body temperature (poikilothermia, for the fancy medical term). And finally, drive his chair onto the special lock mechanism installed where the front passenger seat had been and strap down the back wheels to limit jostling.

It is not quite like a baby's car seat, but neither is it completely dissimilar.

The time delays didn't stop there. We couldn't drive certain streets, as we quickly learned that the potholes or railroad bumps were simply too difficult to handle. After all, when you can't brace yourself and your mobility—and agency—is tied up with being in the exact right position to reach your controls, being pushed out of place by a bumpy road is a significant issue. According to him, going over these bumps also hurt.

There were times when hitting a big pothole would jar him so much that we'd need to pull over, readjust, and rest. His body often needed a sabbath partway through a drive across town.

When I was learning to drive, the four-way stop one mile south of our house was the great divider of the city for me. If I was headed to church, I'd turn right. For school, I'd go straight ahead. And for nearly anything else, it was left to the highway. Driving with my dad, though, the left became an impasse. The railroad tracks that separated our neighborhood from the highway that ran down the center of the city, dividing east from west, were simply too bouncy for a vehicle that was lowered to accommodate a ramp and a person who could not brace or adjust himself. The railroad may as well have been a brick wall when he was in the car. And so, we'd have to take a slightly slower back route to wherever we needed to go, adding even more time to an already lengthy journey.

In her essay, Samuels goes further, acknowledging that crip time isn't just about poor road conditions or complicated processes for buckling in a person in a wheelchair. It is a form of *time travel*, not just *travel time*. As she notes, some disabled people experience at young ages what we often think of as the problems of old age. The most common age-related disabilities are mobility struggles, hearing loss, vision loss, and immunosenescence (the dysregulation of the immune system, making one more susceptible to disease and cancer). These symptoms just happen as we grow old, and although some people will continue to lead active lives, eventually we all lose the resilience of youth.

Except "eventually" is a loaded term, an expectation that simply isn't true for many.

FOR EVERYTHING, THERE IS A SEASON

"Eventually" implies that there is a standard progression to life, in which we start as helpless babies and grow into strong, powerful adults who "eventually" return to a state of physical and mental helplessness. "Eventually" implies that this happens only after a long life of moving about the world with ease.

This same assumption is held in a different key when thinking about when a loved one might pass away. As the youngest of five kids, all of whom were in good health throughout childhood and adulthood, my father could reasonably assume that he would outlive not only his parents, but his siblings as well. It wasn't something named, to my knowledge, and it wouldn't really have been a foregone conclusion given how close in age they all are, but in general we tend to expect that those born first will die first. "First in, first out," as my business professors would remind me.

As anthropologist Andrew Irving notes, chronic illness or disabling accidents can speed up this process for some, and not for others.[2] As cliché as it may sound, no one is promised tomorrow, neither by virtue of being born more recently nor by past health. A car crash doesn't care what your cholesterol levels are and can still disable you if you've never been sick a day in your life. And a world with COVID is still a world with breakthrough infections even for those who are up-to-date on vaccines, diligent with masks, and not in one of the many high-risk categories.

But when expectations that our bodies will be like they are for any length of time are ripped from under us, whether it is because of a new diagnosis, an accident, or just a recognition that a body isn't physically keeping up with what we expect from it, it can be jarring. A new wrinkle, a new jiggle, a bald spot, a slower 5k pace; whatever it is, if you aren't prepared for your body to change, it can be emotionally tough. Even more so when we cannot attribute these changes to age or those changes cause significant disruptions to our daily lives.

As someone who struggles with signed languages despite multiple attempts at learning, and who has been deeply impacted by both the intricate harmonies of Brian Wilson's music and powerful hymn sings, imagining losing my hearing feels like both a loss in what I can *do* and a loss of who I *am*. My expectation is that I will one day lose my hearing to age. But I know, from friends who have lost hearing early in life, some to genetic realities and others to outside factors, that hearing well until old age is simply not a given, as much as I wish it could be.

Disability brings the end-of-life function losses to life all across the timeline. There is no standard for how our bodies behave, but we still carry assumptions. Disability breaks those assumptions, shattering the illusion that we can know, or even control, what our lives will look like. When the tension between my expectations and the reality of life starts to feel overwhelming, it helps to revisit two of my favorite Scriptures.

The first, Matthew 6:25–31, is frequently labeled "Do Not Worry":

For this reason I say to you, do not be worried about your life, as to what you will eat or what you will drink; nor for your body, as to what you will put on. Is life not more than food, and the body more than clothing? Look at the birds of the sky, that they do not sow, nor reap, nor gather crops into barns, and yet your heavenly Father feeds them. Are you not much more important than they? And which of you by worrying can add a single day to his life's span? And why are you worried about clothing? Notice how the lilies of the field grow; they do not labor nor do they spin thread for cloth, yet I say to you that not even Solomon in all his glory clothed himself like one of these. But if God so clothes the grass of the field, which is alive today and tomorrow is thrown into the furnace, will He not much more clothe you? You of little faith! Do not worry then, saying, "What will we eat?" or "What are we to drink?" or "What are we to wear for clothing?" (vv. 25–31)

Matthew 6, to me, is about control as much as worry. Worry isn't a major issue in my life. In fact, I've been accused of not having a single anxious bone in my body—particularly true when leading a youth group or planning an event. Some may argue (and have) that my lack of anxiety makes *others* far more anxious. Part of it may be my willingness to improv and think on the fly, but another part is simply not having a ton of foresight into what might go wrong. And part of it, although not as much as it should be, comes from trusting God to be bigger than the issues I'm dealing with.

Jesus's words in Matthew help me remember that controlling my food or my clothes, or even my words, ultimately doesn't help me grow closer to God. Control doesn't help me learn to lean into the chaos of life. Control doesn't give me the space I need to let God be God.

Understanding the fragile nature of "abled" versus "disabled," especially as the terms relate to God, helps me process that much better what it means to accompany. Very often, our world wants to draw a distinction between who gives support and who receives it. It is commendable to give generously, and hard to avoid pity when you receive charity. But in Matthew 6, God tells us that we all receive generous charity! Caregiving can tempt us to see ourselves as generous, self-sacrificial angels, suffering the indignity of supporting a parent with early-onset Alzheimer's when we really deserve to be traveling, or bearing the weight of a child with an intellectual disability when we ought to be planning for college visits. But no one is given such certainty in life, and none of us are ever actually in control of what shape our lives take. True accompaniment requires us to be openhanded and aware that the division between "abled caregiver" and "disabled care receiver" is a lot more flimsy than we might admit.

My other favorite passage, Isaiah 40, is decidedly less likely to be hanging in a megachurch coffee shop. The flowers and birds of Matthew 6, such lovely images, evoke a sense of serenity and peace. But Isaiah has an edge, a rough hardness to the poetry found in the prophet's words.

> "Comfort, comfort My people," says your God.
> "Speak kindly to Jerusalem;
> And call out to her, that her warfare has ended,
> That her guilt has been removed,
> That she has received of the LORD's hand
> Double for all her sins."
>
> The voice of one calling out,
> "Clear the way for the LORD in the wilderness;
> Make straight in the desert a highway for our God.
> Let every valley be lifted up,
> And every mountain and hill be made low;
> And let the uneven ground become a plain,
> And the rugged terrain a broad valley;
> Then the glory of the LORD will be revealed,
> And all flesh will see it together;
> For the mouth of the LORD has spoken."
> A voice says, "Call out."
> Then he answered, "What shall I call out?"
> All flesh is grass, and all its loveliness is like the flower
>   of the field.

The grass withers, the flower fades,
When the breath of the LORD blows upon it;
The people are indeed grass!
The grass withers, the flower fades,
But the word of our God stands forever.
                              —Isaiah 40:1–8

When people need comfort, it is because they are *uncomfortable* for some reason. Isaiah is speaking a word of love to a people unsettled by warfare, violence, and destruction. In some ways, they brought this on themselves. In other ways, it was far beyond their own hands. Either way, this time of great disruption was filled with the same violent inversions of the expected timeline that disability accompaniment draws out; the subjugation of people always entails embodied hardship. Famine, war-related injuries leading to disabling conditions early in adulthood, children forced to forgo childhood or killed before their own parents: these may be universal across human history, but warfare most certainly brings them to the surface.

Isaiah is offering a word of care to his fellow sufferers. Not exactly the same way that Jesus in Matthew reminds us that God is caring for us because we matter *so much*, even more than the birds of the air. Rather, Isaiah offers comfort from the opposite direction, saying that God cares for us by giving us something so much bigger than ourselves. Indeed, when we know ourselves to be less important, we begin to see that we ourselves will fade, wither, and die, disappearing from the face of the earth, one day to be forgotten by anyone who knew us, who knew our stories, relegated to a faded name on a tombstone or a line on a genealogical report no one will read. And that sounds scary and nihilistic. But it is also freeing.

Because what stands is not our own lives. Our own lives are messy and broken and beautiful and complex and filled with love and joy and regret and failures and successes. But they don't last. And so it doesn't matter so much that everything aligns perfectly. We don't have to worry about losing function, being disrupted by illness or disability, because our lives are ultimately going to be forgotten in the annals of history. We will surely wither and fade, whether our days are filled with arguing with a memory-challenged parent, whether our children need to diaper us and wipe drool from our mouth, or whether our mothers will outlive us.

Later in her essay, Samuels notes that crip time is also *broken time*. "It requires us to break in our bodies and minds to new rhythms, new patterns of thinking and feeling and moving through the world. It forces us to take breaks, even when we don't want to, even when we want to keep going, to move ahead."[3] The expected march through life, with our worth and value stemming from how well we keep ourselves on track with this misguided notion of "normal development," breaks down when confronted with disability. Not just in the bodies of those who actually experience disability, but in those whose lives cannot be divorced from them. To live in true accompaniment with disability, even as someone whose life looks a whole lot like the "standard," is to become attuned to the brokenness of life in ways that are transformative, generative, and, ultimately, comforting.

Disability is a gift that allows us to deal with the realities in front of us, rather than focus on the expectations for what the future ought to hold. Our futures are passing away, withering, fading, just as our lives are. We are free from the burden of being perfect and free from the fear of time being disrupted. One day, all that will stand is the Word of the Lord, a place where we find ourselves held eternally in comfort.

> The glory of the Lord will be revealed,
> And all flesh, disabled and not, disrupted and not,
>   expected and not, will see it together.

WHAT DO YOU SAY TO GRIEF?

Given our assumptions about the "natural order" of things, I had long held the expectation that I would attend my father's funeral. Before his accident, it seemed likely, but far off and abstract. After the accident, though, I knew it was only a matter of time before any one of the many complications from being paralyzed would shut down his body.

I knew what people would say to me when they came up to me in the receiving line, because I said those same things to people when I went to funerals for their loved ones.

I keep a few quick one-liners on deck for funeral receiving lines, just to be prepared. If I didn't really know the person who died, I would say, "I'm so sorry for your loss," which is the most generic way you can show that you aren't a heartless monster. "It's nice seeing all these people here; it was obvious how much they were loved" is another good comment to have in your back pocket. It isn't so generic that everyone says it, but it also doesn't really say anything. The other cliché things, like "Bob was such a wonderful person" and "Jane was so lovely," are a bit dicier, as they can lead to a follow-up, "Oh, how did you know Bob?" or "What was your favorite thing about Jane?" These questions are traps. They want you to distill an entire person's life into a single, poignant statement but they also want to keep things moving and finish these ritual conversations that they won't remember, all while a stream of people presses in, rushing you.

These statements may be canned, easy, and trite. But they are also important. They matter, not because the string of words is some magic balm that makes things OK. There is no incantation that makes a funeral not suck. But there are boring, expected words that bring comfort into a time of pain.

In the midst of a loss, you don't want someone coming up with a wild theory about how AI will re-create loved ones out of brain scans. It might be interesting, but no one wants to learn something at a funeral; all they want is to be reminded of the truths they already know.

When we lose someone, we want to be affirmed that it hurts. We want someone to acknowledge that nothing can make it better, so the best thing to do is to not try. Mark yourself as present, acknowledge where the primary grief lives, and don't be cute. A canned statement, something quick, gets you through the line quickly but also indicates to the grieving family that you *get* it. You get that you can't *get* their pain. You get that you can't fix it or enter into it or help them through it, but still you came and still you said *something*, and *that* is what matters.

I don't always know if what I'm saying is the *thing* I'm supposed to be saying, though. It's one of the hardest aspects of providing pastoral care for me, which I suppose is ironic given that I've been a congregational minister and a hospital chaplain for several years. You'd think I'd have learned by now. The problem is, in those settings, people want authenticity *some* of the time and they want the social ritual *other* times. One skill of the chaplain is to know when someone just wants a pat on the arm and a reading of Psalm 23, and when someone wants to dive deep into the waters of spiritualized self-reflection.

As a caregiver, and thus someone who has to navigate being on both sides of this, knowing what you actually need is a skill few are given the space to hone. Pastors and elders may want to check in, offering a word of comfort, a reminder of Scripture, or just space for a breath. Do you know in that moment if you want a canned statement, just to know that they showed up? Or do you need to sit with a therapist and dive deep into the questions of why me, why them, why now? It is worth taking some time, even as sparse as it often is for caregivers, to listen to your needs. There is absolutely nothing wrong with telling someone, especially a chaplain, exactly what you need from them, whether it is an expected, standard script or a more therapeutic dive into theology.

It's a bit like how in much of Europe, restaurant waitstaff generally leave you alone. You are seated, handed a menu, and then ignored. If you want to order, you have to get someone's attention. And if you want to pay, you often need to flag someone down. One night, while visiting Paris with my mother in her first trip since my dad's death, we sat for hours drinking Aperol at a small restaurant near the Jardin du Luxembourg, nearly by mistake. Each time we were ready for the bill, the staff was nowhere to be found. By the time they made an appearance, we had recovered enough for another round! In America, it's a bit different. Waitstaff are much more likely to come up regularly, and even leave a bill on the table shortly after the food has arrived. Neither of these customs is wrong, but it's nice to know what to expect.

Knowing these scripts can be incredibly helpful when people are looking for support. The philosopher Jacques Derrida notes that death is the experience of the survivors failing to get any response from their loved one. There is comfort in being responded to, and this cuts both ways. When you feel utterly lost as a caregiver, like you have absolutely nothing left, it can be a balm just to say "hello" to a stranger, if only to receive a "hello" back. That little bit of normalcy is sometimes just enough to carry us through a bit longer. It reminds us that we are, for all our challenges, still here. To die is to leave without responding to the cultural conventions of call and response, to leave one hanging, as it were. And so, at funerals, we walk through the lines, we shake the hands, we offer the hugs, we say "he was a good man" and "he sure was" not because it is a magical balm to an overwhelmed and mourning soul but because in the response itself we affirm that we are indeed still alive. Wounded, but alive.

Ritual is important. Having canned responses and questions and comments is actually good, even if it seems inauthentic. Authenticity is an idol. Who gives a shit about authenticity when you just want to quickly acknowledge that it's good for someone to be there but that you don't need them to make things better or say anything at all. We just want to affirm that the call has a response, that we are still here.

Of course, a funeral also brings out theology. Some people always reach for some divine platitude, likely out of habit, while others take earnest solace in a faithful hope. I knew in advance I would want to push back against certain things that would be said, but also that I wouldn't. It would disrupt the ritual. No one wants to learn anything at a funeral.

"Guess he doesn't need his chair anymore. Now he's running around heaven."

"He's finally free."

"I bet he's hiking around somewhere now that he has his legs back."

As if there is some ideal body he has. As if at some point in his time he was peak John. As if he could sacrifice learning things like patience and letting life draw on a longer, more stretchy timeline, in exchange for things like playing tennis or riding bikes. As if we can look at his life and determine which events made him *him* and which events helped erode him. As if the *he* who was before the accident ceased to be, and the *he* who was after the accident was some poor stand-in, a warm body filling the room until he could finally die and be reunited with the legs he was supposed to have. What a way to dismiss a decade of life.

Accompanying my father in life, and in death, means being shaped by his unique relationship with time. His body time traveling from infancy to adulthood and, in some ways, back again. My own life is now marked by the tension between the expectations of time and the acknowledgment that timelines are never set in stone. But however difficult it can be, both practically and emotionally, when you accompany someone enough to travel those timelines alongside them, the Spirit opens new possibilities of engaging with God's timing. God doesn't need us to progress through life in a certain order for us to be full participants in the kingdom; going through life with someone whose daily life serves as a rejection of a straightforward arc offers us the freedom to reject time's domination over our own lives, too.

Some caregivers contend with a broken expectation of what life would look like, particularly those raising children with congenital disabilities. They had hopes and beliefs about the general shape of life that they'd see, and those were dashed when a diagnosis came. Or perhaps that happened later, with the development of an addiction. A friend of mine is unexpectedly dealing with caretaking for her young adult son now, at a time when she expected he would have moved out on his own, because his alcoholism and mental illness make it unsafe for him to live independently. Her expectations for his life, and therefore her own life as well, were shown to be out of step with reality. Somehow, then, her task is to lay down those expectations and acknowledge them as false idols that never held real power. She has found a new acceptance through her unexpected caregiving that God never stated that all twenty-four-year-olds definitely move out and become independent, and now she is free to discover what God has really promised.

It is far easier, however, to simply dismiss disabilities and death as random events that hold no meaning. They just occur when specific events, primarily outside our control, align in particular ways. Your child is autistic? Random genetic variance, probably. Car crash left you paralyzed? Random chance, that other car could have hit anyone. Macular degeneration? Multiple sclerosis? Dementia? Dyslexia? Random, random, random, random.

Of course, if we say that, it's quite easy to make the jump to control them. The world is chaotic and must be tamed. When we invite people to disability conferences, we pigeonhole them into *parent* or *disabled*, controlling their narratives to make it easier for us to decide how to treat them, what to anticipate, what language to use. When we look at disabilities scientifically, medically, or even politically, control can look like eradication, eliminating the possibility of natural diversity. As a general rule, we love to try to exert control over the randomness of life, however we can. And that means, sometimes, rejecting the reality of someone's life in favor of a simple vision of them "restored" to what we're more comfortable with.

But there is something about disability that simply does not reduce to chaos or randomness. Nor does it reduce to God's puppeteering, nor any singular and universal narrative.

When we dwell on an ideal body, or an ideal way of being in the world, this ideal sense of who the person will be for all of eternity, we miss something major about how God is at work in our lives. When I catch a glimpse of the Spirit at work, it sure doesn't seem like she is moving me back toward some moment in my early thirties when I set my personal best for a half marathon, or back at twenty-eight when I had a slight hint of a six-pack in preparation for my wedding and honeymoon. The Spirit has been so active in guiding me toward patience, love, self-sacrifice, and gentleness since I had kids; shouldn't my "ideal" body be the one that has learned to rock a fussy child to sleep, or the one that can now sit in peace with a vomiting toddler through the night, or one that has developed a mind for silly bedtime stories?

Disability so often forces us to center the body, and time, in ways that are limiting and small. As if what God intended for our lives was to have a certain percentage of body fat, or a particular color to our hair, or 20/20 vision, or even two legs and the capacity to run. Our bodies are so much more than that. So what are we saying about our loved ones? Have our words betrayed a belief that they were more complete at some point, that now they are broken or lost in a way that disregards their current life? Our language can bring life or death, and it is our choice how to view care needs and disabilities.

The story we so often tell ourselves is that we need to look a certain way, or follow some external timeline, and that once we get to that ideal our lives will be somehow complete. We likely know it's not true, but the story gets shared over and over anyway, and eventually it becomes an expectation. We need a new social story, a new script that can help us challenge the belief that somewhere out there is a perfect body. A new script that says, "No matter his form, he was beloved."

Hiking History

As a child I was lucky to have interesting natural areas around our home that my parents let me freely explore. My work also instilled in me a love for environments that contained hills, mountains, and other tortuous terrains. So it was no surprise years later when I planned family trips that included hiking and experiencing the outdoors. Given the constraints of family life, our hikes were necessarily short. However, I had nagging desires to go on longer hikes.

The Great Smoky Mountains National Park consists of a large ridge. The apex of this ridge lies from the southwest to the northeast. Approximately halfway from either end of the park there is a mountain pass called Newfound Gap. The main road in the park, Newfound Gap Road, runs from north to south and crosses over the pass. Midway from the north edge of the park to Newfound Gap is a unique geologic formation. It is relatively narrow and rises about 3,000 feet from its base. Because the formation is relatively isolated, the view from the top is spectacular. From this vantage point one can see almost the entire northwest quadrant of the over 800-square-mile park.

As a result this formation, appropriately named Chimney Tops, is a popular hiking destination.

About ten miles from Chimney Tops exists another popular park destination, Mount LeConte. The second highest peak in the Smokies, it can be accessed via one of four trails. The most popular trail is the Alum Cave Trail, which is a relatively short (five-mile), steep, challenging hike. At the summit, hikers will discover the "Cracker Barrel of the Mountains," including cabins for overnight stays, a restaurant for lodgers, and a visitors' center offering a place for folks to hang out and souvenirs for sale.

These two park destinations, Chimney Tops and Mount LeConte, provide the bookends for my hiking history. The former enticed me to further explore this unique natural area and the other resulted in a more ominous outcome.

On one particular trip to the Great Smoky Mountains National Park, I climbed Chimney Tops with my eldest child, Emily, and youngest, Topher. The Chimney Tops trail is very steep, narrow, and rocky. At the base of the trail to Chimney Tops, a sign notes that hikers should expect to commit three hours in order to reach the summit. The three of us walked fairly fast, took no breaks, and arrived in just over thirty minutes! This early success, combined with my desire to hike more, motivated me to plan some dedicated hiking trips.

The first of these trips saw me and my wife Cherry visiting the Lodge at Buckberry Creek, located just outside Gatlinburg, Tennessee. During the daytime, Cherry and I would take short walks and visit the stores in town. Because I wanted a more extensive hiking experience, I left Cherry about 2 one morning and walked the Appalachian Trail until sunrise. A headlamp lit my way until it was no longer needed. On my way back I encountered several rangers beginning their day with a "walk around." They were very impressed with my initiative, and this served as the earliest entry in my hiking portfolio.

Upon our return home I visited a local hiking store called the Top Spot. Cherry thought my expenditure of over $1,200 for backpacking equipment was a bit excessive. I considered it an investment in recreation and exercise. After all, in one fell swoop I was able to buy a quality lightweight backpack, tent, sleeping bag and pad, Gore-Tex rain jacket, small butane burner, and other sundry items. My old equipment was far too outdated and insufficiently lightweight to be of any use whatsoever. Clearly, weight is of the utmost concern for serious hikers like myself.

At first I had the idea of taking backpacking trips that would be about a week or so long. In the Great Smoky Mountains National Park, there are a number of little wooden shelters, and it is about a day hike between each of them. I thought I could perhaps cover around one hundred miles in a single trip, using these shelters as my designated overnight spots. Of course, situations change—especially in national parks. My first attempt was on October 9, 2007. You may recall this date as the beginning of one of the largest stock market crashes in history. My hiking trip was equally calamitous in my life, which says something about the amount of stock I didn't own. The first day, I barely made it to the shelter before sunset. The food I had brought was mostly spoiled, I developed blisters on both of my feet, and I was plagued by persistent leg cramps. After a miserable night, I returned to my vehicle and decided that there must be a better way.

After some research, I decided to do day hiking. This method involved finding a comfortable motel to sleep in at night.

3

Economy

God Reveals Our Worth

Twenty reusable nappies: £220. Backup boxes of newborn and one-month disposable nappies: £30. Secondhand cot with new mattress: £30. Box of baby books: £5. Tapestry to hang in the nursery: £6. Three swaddles: £8. Anti-colic bottles, two-pack: £18. Car seat: £132. Monitor: £100. Muslins: £9. Nappy bin: £10. An irresistible snowsuit that makes your baby look like a squishy panda, even though it's May and you have no idea what size he'll be when it actually snows: £12. It goes on and on and on. And it adds up and up and up.

Two baby stores went bankrupt during our sixth month of pregnancy (hello, closing sales), my wife managed to snag every incredible deal off Facebook Marketplace, and we *still* spent several hundred pounds on the baby well before they made their way to this side of the womb. It's not for nothing that we link babies and economics. Babies are, after all, expensive. But the way we think about this is all wrong.

Babies aren't expensive because they require a significant number of items, many of which are very expensive (and many of which are very adorable, which makes purchasing them sting a tiny bit less). Babies are expensive because they quite literally take every single ounce of every single thing that you have. I mean, sure, a baby doesn't want my old running shoes, but all the same I can't actually keep them for myself. Or at least, if they were demanded as a sacrifice to the gods of baby vomit, I'd have to be willing to part with them. More so, I have to account for the fact that this tiny new human isn't exactly suited for going out on a jog with me and can't be left alone while I churn out some miles.

Do the people we accompany want our new running shoes? Probably not. But do they dictate, thanks to their reliance on us, when and where we can run? Absolutely. That's not showing up in an expense report, but it's definitely a cost.

Culturally, it is easier to accept the unequally weighted economics of life with babies than with most disabled loved ones; we give all that we have, no conditions, just because the very presence of a baby demands it without reservation. A baby has gifts, yes, and that is joyous and fun, but a baby has demands, and those are very often not fun. Our social structure usually tells us that this dynamic is good—we see parents and babies as "normal" and "good," whereas other caregiving situations are typically deemed "tragic" or "unfortunate."

When it is an aging parent, or an alcoholic young adult, or a quadriplegic spouse, we often have less support. The world doesn't see those relationships as normal and good, not like we tend to do with babies and parents. The world needs to acknowledge that caregiving is a wide, diverse, and complex act, involving rearing babies, befriending needy neighbors, parenting aging parents, and so many other situations that emerge in life.

Parents aren't off the hook, either, of course. The world doesn't always give them a very fair experience, with all sorts of competing demands placed on parents that are, frankly, impossible to maintain. More so, there is a theology of parenting and caregiving that insidiously snakes its way into our minds, unless the church can be clearer about what is really happening when we accompany one another through life's needs.

For Christians, there is a serious temptation to look at all the demands of caregiving and use it to pretend that we are like God looking down at our lowly, helpless loved ones. When I put my caregiving relationship into an analogy that flatters my sacrifices, I can imagine being God. I see my child making bone-headed mistakes that I've made hundreds of times already, and I extend grace and love because their presence simply demands it. I see my spouse suffering and I run a bath, massage their hands, guide them down the steps, grin and bear it when they say something crass in public, and drive them to their doctor's appointments.

"Look at me, rocking this crying baby at 3 a.m.; look at me sacrificing my own vacation time to care for my mother with dementia. Look at how gracious I am! Look how much love I have for this pitiful person who can't offer me anything in return. Truly, I am like God, accompanying this broken and weak person. How unselfish and holy of me!"

This is, of course, a horrendous analogy. The directionality is all off; when I look at one of my children or someone I accompany, I am *not* God looking down at my hapless creation; I am instead staring into the very face of God. God is not in the mighty and powerful who extend grace to the weak. Matthew 25:31–46 tells us that it is the hungry, the homeless, the imprisoned, the weak, who truly embody the Lord. The poor and weak, the very body of Jesus, invite us to accompany them in their unapologetic neediness, and in so doing reshape both us and the world.

The tendency to infantilize disabled people makes them ripe for abuse within this mind-set, perhaps even more so than babies. True accompaniment resists this narrative, instead forcing us to contend with what concepts of weakness and neediness really mean. As theologian Deborah Creamer reminds us, disability is a sociopolitical category that describes the universal experience of being *limited*.[1] To truly participate in the mystery and presence of God, according to Roberto Goizueta, those who inhabit positions of power—parents, students at a top-ranked research university, the wealthy, able-bodied caregivers, whoever—are invited to step out from their spaces of comfort and authority to encounter God's transcendent-yet-present mystery.[2]

When you comfort a sick toddler, when you make a cozy and safe nursery to welcome a newborn, or when you let the needs of a disabled loved one supersede your own desires, you aren't playing God. You are seeing God before you. And you are being discipled, formed for a life that is more gentle, peaceful, loving, graceful, and slow. You are, through your accompaniment, being radically re-created.

But the tendency to deify ourselves is far more common, from what I can tell.

When I lived in Nashville, this view that the dad of the family is basically God was common enough in the church where I worshiped that I started avoiding services led by particular ministers. I knew the sermon was going to start with some analogy based on their experience of fatherhood, which would magically have happened that week while they were meditating on Scripture. Their kid would make a mistake and the father would forgive them; the kid wouldn't want to do something difficult but the father knew it was in their long-term best interest, etc., etc., ad nauseam.

I think sometimes pastors like this assume that the word "father" should always be capitalized, no matter who it refers to.

I met my chronically unhoused friends thanks to my disgust with one such sermon. After hearing the initial pitch at the start of the sermon ("While I was praying through these Scriptures and asking God what he was trying to show me, my little three-year-old had this meltdown in Target . . ."), I got up and left.

I didn't go home, though. I wanted to stay for the remainder of worship, including the truly excellent Communion bread. The recipe, I later found out, included some unbelievable amount of butter, plus a little honey, so I think I was justified in waiting it out. So I hung out on the front steps. While I was out there, I saw a couple off to the corner, smoking. It was pretty clear immediately that these two were part of Nashville's sizable unhoused population.

Sean and Ellie were living in a motel, paying week to week.

They had been in and out of shelters, spent time in tents, and were church members. They had been in trouble a few times for asking for money in the service, and the church office was trying to find an appropriate and safe way to help them without being taken advantage of. But like many people who have been left behind by the formal systems of care that both the church and state like to pretend are working, they were at times out of sync with social expectations. They sometimes said words that weren't "church appropriate." They sometimes didn't smell very clean. OK, they always smelled, but they didn't exactly have extra money for laundry, so what would you expect? There weren't any washing machines available at the church; clean clothes were important enough to serve as a basis for judgment, but not important enough to provide.

They needed rides to get around the city, and rather than tapping some buttons on their phones to command a driver to meet them and deliver them to wherever they wanted while they sat silently in the back, they just asked people. Like, actual people. For a real favor. At church. Unbelievable, right?

Sean and Ellie were outside the church because they were taking a smoke break. I was outside because I was taking a bad-theology break. I think in my righteous anger toward yet another frustrating sermon, I was more inclined to see them as Christ does—beloved and wondrous, even if misunderstood and condemned by the well-off and tragically hip pre-suburban crowd inside. We vented our mutual frustrations and talked about who Jesus was if not an upper-middle-class dad wrangling kids in a Target, and I gave them a lift to their motel.

This was the start of a long relationship. Not one that was always safe, or easy, or even healthy. But it was a real relationship, with all the complexity that comes with it. In a sense, it was a caregiving relationship. It probably shouldn't have been, to be honest. Rather, in an ideal world, it would have been one of mutuality and equity. There is nothing wrong with being a caregiver or care receiver, but not every relationship ought to be cast in those terms.

The temptation—like parents seeing themselves in the God

role—is to say that I became like God to these needy and lowly poor folk. That I was their savior in their time of need. That they just needed to ask and I'd deliver for them. But really, it was a struggle to be their friend. They'd call me most days, usually to ask a big favor or to come see me. It was always couched in a "we're just about to make a big change and get back on our feet" kind of way, as if I was the one missing ingredient to what would make their lives stable again. It often felt really high pressure, and often they'd ask for a little cash. After the first day, I told them I couldn't give them cash and could rarely buy them food.

I was a grad student living in a co-op and working three jobs while still accruing debt, so I wasn't exactly rolling in the dough. But I was also a grad student at Vanderbilt living in the very posh neighborhood known as Midtown Nashville, so I had plenty of privileges well beyond the number in my bank account. I mean, Taylor Swift owned a penthouse condo next door to us. But I shared a kitchen with twenty other students and regularly went to guest lectures solely for the free snacks. I had a foot in each world.

Sometimes I'd ignore my phone and pretend not to see their missed calls. If I was their savior, I was pretty shitty at it. I did try to connect them with bigger resources, and I did try to offer what I could, but I am not Jesus. I am not God. They were not my children. And even then, having children does not make me some prefiguration of the Lord. If anything, they were more gracious to me than I was to them.

Being friends with chronically unhoused folks—like having kids or a disabled loved one—does expose us to more of the nature of Christ, though. Not because being a caregiver, in whatever capacity, helps us see what it must be like for God to see us, but because every single thing in this world should be pointing us to something true about God. Nothing, absolutely nothing, is neutral or devoid of theological meaning. A child *means* something. Having friends who are needy and overbearing and smell like smoke and unwashed clothes *means* something, even if what it means is that I am more selfish than I want to admit and sometimes my selfishness directly causes others to suffer. That has theological depth, even if I don't want it to. To accompany someone is always going to present a challenge. It will demand something from us.

BEING A TRUE GIFT

Babies are amazing, wonderful, fun, delightful, and astounding. If I could have a superpower, it would be to look at everyone the way I look at babies. Well, actually if I got to pick a superpower, it would be to manipulate the coefficient of friction (Bad guys running away? Now the floor is like ice!), but a close second would be the ability to look at adults the way I look at babies. Like babies, adults have gifts. They can be beautiful and awe-inspiring. And just like babies, adults have demands, too.

While I was ducking sermons and accompanying Sean and Ellie through life, I also led a ministry for adults with intellectual disabilities (IDD).[3] When it comes to adults with IDD, we love to focus on gifts. That helps us get inspired, feeling so good about the way someone else managed to live in spite of incredible hardship, and most importantly that *we* don't have to be like *them*. A focus on gifts alone takes away all the nuance and drama from real life and lets the nondisabled write off the experience of intellectually disabled people, ignoring their demands for friends, financial autonomy, and independent living, shifting our gaze to a simple story about being loving or being content.

Stella Young, a disability advocate, offered a helpful reminder in her TED Talk "I'm Not Your Inspiration, Thank You Very Much," that stories cannot be so readily flattened. It is worth quoting her at length:

> These images [of disabled people "overcoming" their hardships], there are lots of them out there, they are what we call inspiration porn. And I use the term porn deliberately, because they objectify one group of people for the benefit of another group of people. So in this case, we're objectifying

disabled people for the benefit of nondisabled people. The purpose of these images is to inspire you, to motivate you, so that we can look at them and think, "well, however bad my life is, it could be worse. I could be that person. . . ." I am not here to inspire you. I am here to tell you that we have been lied to about disability. Yeah, we've been sold the lie that disability is a Bad Thing, capital B, capital T. It's a bad thing, and to live with a disability makes you exceptional. It's not a bad thing, and it doesn't make you exceptional.[4]

The word "porn" is jarring, but apt. We can be inspired by someone, certainly, just like you can be physically attracted to someone in a healthy and respectful way. But porn is a way of objectifying someone else for our own use. Just as sex is a good and wonderful thing when shared in a healthy, equitable relationship with appropriate boundaries, inspiration is a real, wonderful thing in the right circumstances. But forcing someone into a small story that we use for ourselves, not allowing them to control their own narrative, turns them into objects that we get to consume. The gifts of other people become mere products for us.

Alternatively, if we don't want to look at their gifts and use them as fodder for our own inspiration, we tend to try to blot them out entirely. This is the basis of eugenics. If we can't use someone, we'd rather they simply not exist. Letting folks exist in their full diversity challenges us to see their gifts as blessings from God with equal value to our own. This can be a struggle when our identities are often built on being better than someone else. Likewise, the fullness of human diversity forces us to acknowledge that some people are marginalized within the world we make.

It can be hard to study people's lives through the lens of "margins" and "oppression." For one, it can be emotionally challenging; sometimes the problems seem too big to deal with, and sometimes we discover ourselves to be part of those problems. It can also be a little reductive and unhelpful to individual needs. Still, looking at the world with an eye toward how laws and social conventions shape us all helps us learn how the world tries to eliminate certain people. The attempt to eliminate disabled people from society is known as eugenics, and it has a long history. The United States approved the legal sterilization of disabled folks for decades thanks to *Buck v. Bell* (1927), a Supreme Court case that has never been overturned. Many states maintained sterilization laws for criminals, eventually limiting it to sexual criminals in theory, but stories of inmates being forcibly sterilized persist, and Louisiana just signed into law the right of judges to sterilize felons convicted of sex crimes against children. Operating on the same logic of eradication, Canada's 2021 broadening of its Medical Assistance in Dying policy not only allows for individuals to request being legally killed by medical professionals, but also has presented death as a valid option to eliminate social support needs for marginal persons.[5]

In 2022, Amir Farsoud learned that he would need to find a new housing situation because his landlord was selling his unit. Aware that the Ontario Disability Support Payment that he relied on for income was insufficient to secure him housing, Farsoud turned to his doctors and asked for assistance in dying. Seeing that Farsoud faced dealing with his disability and chronic pain as a homeless man, and understanding that the government wasn't willing to act as a caregiver, his doctor signed the form "allowing" him to die.[6] The process is different from sterilization, but it is still eugenics; our societies get rid of the people deemed too needy, too aberrant, too different, and too expensive. The willingness of our countries to eradicate the people we find ourselves caring for is a jarring reality, and that disjunction can cause real psychological harm.

We rarely admit that someone's embodiment and presence makes demands on us, especially because we don't like it when our individual rights are impinged upon. How dare this child with nonverbal autism demand we restructure our lives in this way? How dare this quadriplegic demand I move at 3 mph? Better to simply refuse their existence. Wish them away, offer them suicide, prevent them from having kids of their own so that we don't have to deal with more of *those people*.

As part of our IDD ministry practice, we would begin by gathering for a meal before moving on to music, games, a brief word or worksheet on faith, and prayer time. It was a ton of work, a ton of fun, and one of the most formative experiences of my life. Trying to find appropriate ways to teach abstract concepts like "grace" and "God's love" to a group of very diverse learners was hard, but ultimately helped me see where God was active among people whom the traditional church had long forgotten.

One evening, we learned about 1 Corinthians 12 and the discourse on the body being unified but having many different parts. We lay on the ground, all equal and participating together, to form various words spelled out with our bodies. As we made these letters together, we could see how necessary everyone was. Could we have spelled "LOVE" without Marco laying his head next to Cassie's or "CARE" without Rachel's hands on Jake's shoulders? Finding a way to display how we can become the body of Christ was a gift we all enjoyed, and far more meaningful than any sermon or lecture.

It was easy to get folks excited about this ministry, but it was hard to keep the majority of volunteers around. A few dedicated folks made the engine run, and for them I am forever grateful, but we always needed more hands than we had. I tried to help people see that our friends were full people with support needs and gifts all together in one mixed-up bundle. Watching many of them grow deeper in their faith made my own faith flourish.

When you let the diversity of God inspire you, seeing the Spirit active in ways that aren't always welcome in the "big church," you can begin to appreciate moments that might not seem at first blush to be theological at all. Is singing a Taylor Swift song an act of worship? What if it is with a group of friends? What if in that moment, you lose your inhibitions that you normally carry, forgetting to try to make your voice sound good, and instead being fully invested in sharing a moment with friends? What if those friends have been cast aside by society and church alike, finding few outlets for genuine love and friendship, and singing a pop song at the top of your lungs is the only time that month you will get to see your voice swirl into a mighty chorus with people who know you, who love you, who see you? Is God there, in the holiness of accidental harmonies and the breaking of the breaded chicken nuggets? If not, then I'm not sure I know who God is.

But also, sometimes it was incredibly frustrating and, frankly, gross. Aaron, who communicated primarily through grunts and flapping movements, might break the ice by unexpectedly shouting in your face, then giggling. It was always shocking, but somehow lovely. It was, after all, one of his primary methods of communication, and there is something powerful about being invited into a conversation with anyone, whether you are speaking with shared words or not. But Aaron might also unexpectedly sneeze half-eaten chili back into your face and mouth while you tried to support him in eating. It happened to me more than once. It was not very lovely.

There are myriad ways of being a caregiver. Sometimes we might assume that there is only one primary caregiver, and they are the one responsible for the vast majority of hours served. But we have to see that being a caregiver is a role that many of us play, even if it is for a few hours a week rather than all-consuming. For those in the former boat, dealing with the gross realities of toileting and messy feedings daily, the challenge is to remember that 1 Corinthians 12 promises us that we have a part to play, and that all parts are important—especially the gross ones. We need mouths, teeth or gums, saliva, stomach acid, intestines, lots of bile and juicy enzymes, and, yes, even excrement, to transform food into nutrients. Maybe in the midst of a gross situation, when a catheter has failed or when a bowel program has gone awry, when there is someone else's half-chewed food on your shirt, you can reach back to God's word, gently reminding you that most of the parts of a body are pretty gross and absolutely indispensable. The work you do matters so much, even when it is small, seemingly unimportant, or downright yucky.

If you can't take these kinds of moments, the really gross and difficult, and hold them alongside the beautiful, if you can't acknowledge that these *are in fact* the beautiful moments because they are real and authentic and unmediated by programs or money and they were removed from the intention to train and make Aaron into something different, then you aren't experiencing the gift of accompaniment. That was the challenge of this ministry, and why so many volunteers who were so excited at first never lasted very long.

This is the economy of disabilities, that the exchange is not a whole life for a broken one, but a giving up of the need to be something we can never be for the sake of being who we already are. Disabilities, even if much of the time they are difficult and messy and infuriating and painful, have the capacity to be unmediated truths told in action to a world that cannot stand to be anything less than *super*natural.

WHICH BODIES ARE WORTHY?

At the end of his life, my father spent only a few days in hospice after a few days in the intensive care unit (ICU). His lungs were significantly infected, and, frankly, they were too tired to keep going. The nature of his accident meant that certain muscles had to play an outsized role in keeping his body alive, as others no longer performed their earlier functions. This meant that after ten years of added expectations on his diaphragm, any slight respiratory illness was apt to be his last.

It is for this reason that as a family we feel grateful that he died before the advent of COVID-19. Had he lived during that pandemic, he would have been incredibly restricted and isolated as the most vulnerable of the vulnerable. Inevitably, any contact with the disease would have been a death sentence—one we would not have been allowed to accompany him through.

But he died months before the first wave of COVID emerged. He had transferred to the ICU a few times in his final years, and each time it was generally expected that he would make a complete recovery ("complete" meaning a restoration to a still-quadriplegic body, of course). This time, though, in summer 2019, his care team was far less hopeful. Their assumptions about his capacity to recover were bleak enough that I, still living in Scotland at the time, bought a last-minute international flight to be home.

Somewhere in the in-between, when death was looming in the corner but had yet to announce its presence, I sat in a chair in the hospice room and absentmindedly read the news. I was effectively sitting vigil, ready to clang the bells to alert the clan should I hear the death rattling inside my father's weakened throat, but I lacked the focus and patience required to *just be* without doing something else. And so, I read about stories of people I didn't know, and policies that didn't impact me, and politicians making promises that would have been functionally impossible even if they had intended to keep them. As I was reading and keeping a loose vigil over my slowly fading father, in walked a priest.

He was older, likely nearing retirement age, with a small remnant of white hair and a clear display of confidence. He did not acknowledge me, presumably because I was invisible to him. This priest, whose name I still do not know, marched directly up to my father's bed and began to pray, with no introduction or greeting. My instinct, developed not so much as a minister but more so as a child raised to never miss a Sunday church service, was to immediately bow my head and pray along with anyone who begins to pray out loud. It just feels respectful, or at least that is the narrative I have been taught. And yet, what is respectful behavior toward a body who cannot object to being prayed upon?

There are many, like me, who never realized that the power of prayer cuts both ways until they met someone who had been wounded deeply by human attempts at communicating with God. In seminary, a white friend of mine relayed that her father had prayed against her falling in love with a Black man (she did anyway). At the same time, several of my gay friends knew of churches attempting to pray their sexual attractions away. And a huge percentage of my disabled friends experience *regular* attempts by friends and strangers alike to "heal" them of their impairments. How responsible is it to use the language of

God to attempt to name "God's good plan" for someone if it involves asking for a radical transformation of attributes that are not barriers to God's love, like who you love or whether you use a wheelchair? How accurate and loving is it to tell someone by your prayers that the life they know is somehow outside of God's knowing embrace? That if they were a fundamentally different person, God would accept them?

Prayer is power. To be in a position to pray over someone is a privilege, bound by the command to steward our right to speak to God against the desire to turn prayer into some sort of magic code that transforms our environment into our own selfish vision. Don Saliers, a Methodist theologian, claims that prayer and worship are less about making demands on God and more about helping us learn how to describe both God and the world. Theology is a lot like grammar, organizing our faith lives. "Worship and prayer are the rule-keeping activities which keep verbal professions of faith true to their object," helping the faithful actively fight against the sins of hypocrisy, Saliers says.[7]

If prayer time is to be respected, it must be respectful. Praying someone's identity away does not feel very respectful. And praying for someone without so much as a cursory introduction, much less consent, feels like some significant boundary that ought not be crossed, even if the person is in a coma. This does not mean that it is wrong to pray earnestly for the people in your life, even those who do not want prayer, but we must be aware of prayer's capacity to lead us toward sanctification. In worship, God is praised most when people begin to resemble God themselves. You don't pray to *get* something, you pray to *become* something—something more aligned with the person of Christ. That is what glorifies God. Not us getting showered with material gifts and miraculous healings, but becoming more like the person of Christ, who still lives in each of God's children. Prayer is not a secret incantation, nor a Magic 8 Ball, but a means of reshaping ourselves into the people of God.

Would it have killed this priest to pretend my dad was conscious, to say, "Hi there, Mr. Endress, I'm Father So-and-So and I'd like to pray for you today if that is all right?" No. Would it have made some difference to my father, in his comatose state? Almost assuredly not. But it would have made the act of prayer a move toward honoring a full person, even if that full person had very limited brain activity. It would have changed something for *the priest*, shaping his perspective on the value of all God's children, no matter their state of consciousness or ability.

The God I worship cares for those in comas just as much as those celebrating a Super Bowl MVP award or an unexplained physical healing. And my prayers should reflect that, so that I can become the type of person who cares the way my God does, the type of person who cares not about *getting* things or achieving dreams, but *becoming* a better reflection of Christ's body in this world.

This was not the first priest to ignore us in favor of performing some act of supposed worship on my dad, however. In fact, there was a time during my father's initial postaccident rehabilitation when a well-meaning priest nearly killed Dad. The chaplain, in his defense, was making his standard rounds and offering Eucharist to any who desired it. My father was new to the facility, and so when the chaplain poked his head in and asked, "Is he Catholic?" my mother and I said yes, without thinking. He had been baptized Catholic, and I count his side of our family as very positive representations of what faithful life can look like. But the immediate response to hearing my dad's Catholic background was for this chaplain to say, "Oh great, he can receive the Eucharist here."

My mother, his primary caregiver and thus the person most responsible for his safety, was very quick to say, "No, actually, he is on a vent and cannot have food." The chaplain, who I am not accusing of dismissing a woman on a matter of faith and medicine, dismissed her. He continued to make preparations to place a wafer on my dad's tongue, saying something to the effect of "It's small, there's really no issue with dietary complications." Had my mother not intervened, again, as forcefully as she did, or if she had stepped out for any reason before the chaplain's unplanned arrival, there is a significant likelihood that my father would have aspirated the body of Christ and choked to death.

Who owns a body? Do you own yours? What about when you can no longer move your muscles, cannot swallow on your own, cannot breathe on your own? Do chaplains and doctors and nurses have any claim to you? What about your family? The caregivers who accompany you?

The famed case of Terri Schiavo reminds us that these hypothetical questions have real-life implications. In Terri's case, her husband Michael believed the assessment of one side of the medical community, understanding that Terri's heart attack had left her brain dead. But Terri's parents, Robert and Mary Schindler, held a different belief around Terri's status and desires. The resultant court cases, media inquiries, and appeals took seven years to conclude, reaching as high up as the president of the United States, who personally intervened.[8] Who had the right to decide whether Terri wanted to remain on a feeding tube? Her husband? Parents? Doctors? The president?

Terri could not communicate for herself. Who was given ownership of her body as a result? Who was accompanying her in all this?

Or, consider the case of Ashley X, who was born with static encephalopathy. Although she can communicate to some degree, her parents argued that it was in her best interest to remain in their care throughout her life. In an effort to make that possible, they had a hysterectomy performed on her (to prevent menstruation) and the surgical removal of her nascent breast buds (to prevent development). They also used an estrogen therapy that closed her growth plates faster than would have happened naturally. This meant that Ashley would not experience puberty and would remain a small, childlike figure who could be more easily lifted and cared for in a home setting.[9]

Did Ashley have a right to experience the fullness of natural life, even at the expense of her care plan? She could not consent to the removal of her uterus, but then again, neither could she consent to the removal of her appendix, which was also taken as a precaution. After all, she likely wouldn't be able to name her symptoms should she have appendicitis in the future, a potentially life-threatening issue. Is there a moral difference between our organs? Aside from function, what makes a uterus different from an appendix? In cases where those accompanying a disabled person are the legal decision makers, how ought they go about deciding these things?

Saliers is clear that prayer ought to shift us toward becoming the people of God, but he doesn't stop there. Prayer also functions to highlight our thanksgiving for God's good gifts. What gifts does Ashley have that are worth giving thanks over? Which of these moral choices gives her, and her accompanists, the capacity to rejoice in the work of God most authentically?

Most parents assume the care of their kids, full on at first and steadily decreasing as they learn to do more things for themselves: eating, using a toilet, bathing, reading, driving, moving out. And as their kids become adults, they still provide some things, like advice or maybe a financial safety net, but not day-to-day care. This is the standard narrative. But disability disrupts this. Ashley's parents are her caregivers, but with a stretched-out timeline. They can't anticipate a day when she won't rely on them. And so, because they hold to this story of needing to care for her in particular ways until she dies, they were willing to modify her body to make it easier to handle those duties. How might we narrate the notion of *gift* in this account—the gift of modern medicine, making her care easier, versus the gift of the body, given for us, even in the brokenness and pain of life?

Prayer is also *anamnesis*, the remembering of God's work done through the body of Jesus Christ. We often use that term in theological circles when talking about the Eucharist, or Communion, because we intentionally remember the sacrificial work done for Jesus at that moment in a service, but it can really apply to all prayers. We pray to God through Christ, who was not simply a teacher, but a sacrifice; Jesus was not just a spirit, but a body who was broken and killed. Nancy Eiesland, who many consider the first major theologian to intentionally write "disability theology," reminds us that "the foundation of Christian theology is the resurrection of Jesus Christ. Yet seldom is the resurrected Christ recognized as a deity whose hands, feet, and side bear marks of profound physical impairment."[10] To pray in the name of Christ is to remind ourselves Jesus is the connection between heaven and a bodily earth. Jesus is our medium for orienting ourselves toward God, and without Christ's death and resurrection our prayers are adrift. When we pray over the bodies of disabled people and ask for "healing," or fail to see them for their full worth as God's beloved, are we really remembering Christ's loving and sacrificial death?

Broken bodies are not unique to disabilities. Caregivers have specific roles that aid in covering the needs of others, but that doesn't imply that any of us are without limitations and struggles. Too often, we divide people into care receivers and caregivers, or disabled and not disabled. But theologian Deborah Creamer reminds us that everyone is limited in some way, and equally incapable of fully embodying the diversity of human life.[11] It isn't that caregivers are inherently "normal," but rather that we have told ourselves a story about normalcy and disability so often that we have become convinced that only certain people get to experience "wholeness." But the embodiment of Christ, broken on a cross and again with every breaking of the bread in Communion, reminds us that it is in the brokenness that we find God most present.

A Quick Trip

I always called Cherry to check in at the end of a hike. On my October 10, 2010, hike, in which I broke my neck descending the Alum Cave Trail with Topher, I did not call. She was waiting to hear from me, but our family friend Jeff Bosley called her instead. He had come along on this trip to do some fishing and general sightseeing of his own, with the three of us happy to play cards each evening. He was also a willing driver from the motel to the trailheads, which made planning day hikes significantly easier. His presence on the trip was also an untold benefit in the wake of disaster.

Jeff called Cherry and told her that I had fallen on the mountain. He didn't know much except that and Topher and I would be delayed in returning from what was meant to be a long weekend trip. Jeff blew off her immediate fears because he did not yet realize the severity of the accident.

I did not learn quite how these events unfolded until reading the reports that the family had made for my CaringBridge website. I was not in any position to keep track of who was where, and when. Apparently, after he raced down the mountain, Topher had come across Jeff in the parking lot while searching for cell phone reception. Being only three miles from the trail-head, we were within an hour or so of the expected pickup time, and with cell reception being so spotty in the mountains, Jeff didn't want to risk being late. Topher told Jeff that I needed assistance in descending the rest of the way, but didn't want to share much more, so Jeff assumed this was not life-threatening. Neither one had good enough cell phone service to place an emergency call, so Jeff drove a ways down the road while Topher serendipitously encountered some park rangers responding to a completely unrelated call.

Although Jeff's call had indicated to her that the situation was not that serious, Cherry had a premonition that something was wrong and she continued calling for three to four hours without getting an answer.

When they finally connected again, Cherry questioned Jeff in some detail and with growing concern. This time, since Topher had returned as part of the rescue team that carried me down, Jeff finally had further information and told Cherry she would need to be at whatever hospital I was going to end up at, so she needed to get a bag and start driving. Still, he didn't know the extent of my injuries and was hesitant to call it a true emergency. Cherry quickly packed a bag, picked up our two other children, and headed toward Knoxville. After all, I was an experienced hiker and knew how to get down a mountain. If I needed assistance, Cherry knew in her gut that I must be badly injured.

While Jeff was not wrong in trying to prevent an uncertain situation from becoming something unnecessarily panic-inducing, what he could not have known was that a specialized mountain rescue team was en route to secure and transport me down. Had the trail been suitable, they would have flown in a helicopter to save time. By "assistance" with heading down, they meant that I was to be immobilized on a specialized litter, which was a bit like a unicycle with a backboard attached instead of a saddle. They would push, pull, pulley, hoist, and maneuver me down three miles of rocky, steep, slick terrain, taking hours.

After I fell, I immediately knew something was wrong. The first thing out of my mouth was "Go get help." Fortunately,

Topher ran into two rangers at the bottom of the mountain. It seems odd to say, but the fellow hiker who, just before my accident, had fallen into hypoglycemic shock was instrumental in saving my life. Had those rangers not been at the bottom of the trail, who knows how long it would have taken Topher to run down the road until he found a signal? They were able to split their duties, with Ranger Brad accompanying Topher back to me before coordinating a full team rescue.

Apparently, while I was waiting on Topher to return with the rangers, a family of tourists from Japan came across me. Topher had made sure to emphasize that they could not move me, especially my neck, and at one point the little girl, who was reportedly no more than five, offered a cute cartoon bandage for me. Topher felt that they had the understanding and willingness to sit there without moving me, which gave him the freedom to leave for help. Some time later, another hiker on the trail came across me and sat with me. She was a nurse, and she stayed until Topher returned. I do not have a clear recollection of any of them, but on the incredibly slim chance that they find this book, thank you.

Cherry remembers Jeff insisting that things weren't that bad, but she knew they were. I had hurt myself doing a number of silly things many times in the past, like the time I got stuck in the bathtub and almost drowned when I suffered whole body cramps after a taxing tennis tournament (and a lunch consisting of nothing but soda and cherry pie). Some level of spectacular failure was always partly expected. But this situation felt, to everyone involved, far different from the outset.

Cherry's experience was one of dotting her i's and crossing her t's even in the midst of a massively emotional challenge. She was able to call Emily and Michael, our Evansville-dwelling children, to warn them to pack, pick them up, call her sister to sort out caring for the house and dog, label and leave keys for work, and finally—at the corner of the street as she was leaving—manage to call her boss to tell her that she didn't know when she would be returning to town.

She would not see Evansville again for six months.

While she was driving, I was being hoisted down the trail. Immediate medical response is critical to minimizing damage from spinal cord injuries. This is not always possible, depending on where and how the accident occurred. The rescue board, with its singular giant tire and many straps to keep me secure, had to navigate through numerous obstacles. For example, there is one section where the trail runs into the side of a cliff and emerges via a tunnel several hundred feet later (and lower). The backboard would not fit through the tunnel, so they had to build a scaffolding to lift the board over the escarpment. We needed six people at all times to surround the litter, but these trails were not designed for many people to walk side by side. All in all, the rescue took seven hours and fourteen people to move me down the trail to a point where a helicopter could land.

I was alert throughout the seven-hour trek down the mountain, and it wasn't until I got to the helicopter site that I began to break with reality. Even though I was fully conscious while coming down the mountain I was also simultaneously experiencing what is commonly known as a near-death experience.

It is difficult to put into words what I felt during this near-death experience. I didn't "see lights" or experience any other physical manifestations. It was purely an emotional experience. The best way I can explain it is to say that I was in a great mood. I think we all struggle with varying degrees in our beliefs about an afterlife, and my euphoria came about because I intrinsically felt that an afterlife did indeed exist, even though I didn't necessarily feel like I was heading there anytime soon.

The helicopter was waiting for me in the parking lot of the Sugarlands Visitor Center of Great Smoky Mountains National Park. I remember little, but I believe that despite the urgency we made several stops to drop off other passengers. It is hard to tell in a situation like this what the reality was for those not strapped to a board, unable to move their body. Being immobilized can be very disorienting on its own, and on top of that I was dealing with a life-threatening spinal cord injury. These stops that I felt may not have actually happened, but in my state I certainly felt that we were more like a city bus than an emergency helicopter. During each stop I felt that I was getting weaker and weaker and was afraid that I wasn't going to live. At some point I remember someone telling me it was my turn to get off (perhaps this is when I reached the trauma center). At this point, I remember being greatly relieved.

During the helicopter ride, I remember that, in addition to my worries about whether or not I would make it to my destination, I had a sort of waking dream where the helicopter blades were slowly twisting my body in a clockwise direction. In this dream, the helicopter pilot explained to me that each person's body had a limit as to how much torque it could absorb during this lifetime. He explained that many helicopter pilots would reach their maximum torque limit and have to resign. He further explained that I was near my lifetime limit and therefore might not make it to my destination.

Another delusion that I experienced during the helicopter ride ensued when we passed over a large house under construction on the side of a large mountain, though I could not have seen such a sight in the late night darkness, immobilized as I was. I imagined I was in the basement of this house and people were nailing down plywood on the first floor. At some point in time, a woman began removing the boards as fast as the other people were nailing them down. Eventually I escaped this basement trap on the side of the mountain. I suspect that it was my wife, Cherry, who was removing the boards.

I woke up for a short time, alone, strapped to a circle, and realized that I was completely paralyzed. This one was actually real; the circle contraption was a medical device of some sort. Although my family and medical caregivers report that I was alert and talking rationally at times, this is the only truly vivid memory I have of my two-week stay in the University of Tennessee Trauma Center.

4
History
Living Out a Baptismal Promise

Navigating the complexities of my father's medical care gave me the sense that health care must always be viewed with equal parts suspicion and hope. We cannot assume, whether as patients, caregivers, or advocates, that doctors and nurses are anything other than human, capable of making errors in judgment and practice despite their often valiant efforts to minimize harm and act as ethically as they know how. Experiencing the bureaucracies involved, although it was my mother who mostly dealt with these headaches, confirmed in my opinion Niebuhr's great thesis that we are far more likely to sin against one another in social systems than as individuals. Still, there remains a hope that medical care, even when insufficient alone, can assist us in seeing God at work, especially in the lives of those we care for.

When my wife, Sam, and I decided to expand our family, we considered both adoption and biological means. And in both cases, we pondered the possibility of parenting a child with a disability. Given my field of study and my doctoral adviser's specific expertise in disabilities, technology, and medical ethics, we were prepared for questions regarding antenatal testing and screenings. In some countries, these screenings are mandatory. You don't have an option; they simply look for the neural tube opacity and other markers of potential genetic disabilities in utero and advise you on how to proceed based on their findings. Without that knowledge, they reckon, you simply can't make informed decisions on care. The unfortunate result of this has been an increase of selective abortion for disabled babies (or babies presumed to have disabilities).

Restricting access or information doesn't seem like an ideal situation, of course, and there are plenty of horror stories of women experiencing unforeseen complications who must endure extra surgeries and wait times even to remove a nongrowing, non-heartbeat-having fetus, or one that is growing in the fallopian tube rather than the womb. Such children have no possibility of life, yet many women face difficulties accessing basic health care to keep themselves safe. This is a different, yet related, issue from selecting abortions to avoid bearing disabled children. The lack of trust in pregnant people to make the appropriate choices in their own lives as it relates to carrying children with markers of genetic abnormalities, or not, has spilled into other situations that ought to be much more cut-and-dry. This is one instance that illustrates the intersectionality inherent to disabilities as a concept.

Women are the largest group of practicing moral ethicists in the world, given that they have had to navigate the world of child-having and child-raising, each fraught with constant questions about what is right and what it means to have life, and to live it well. Every playtime, every meal, the ins and outs of daily life habituating children to the world are acts with deep moral and ethical significance. As more and more work is shared equally and across gender lines, this becomes work shared by all the adults of a family. But even in today's Western world, in which equality is both the trend and the ideal, most families still assign the labor of teaching ethics to the littlest ones to women.[1] Disproportionately, this bleeds into all forms of caregiving; women are more likely to be tasked with caring for aging parents and disabled spouses, and handling the details of children with unique accommodations.[2] And yet, we typically do not trust women to make ethical decisions on their own.

Even before we conceived, we knew that no test or screening would dictate for us whether our child was worthy of engaging this world. Other than in the extremely sad case of an obviously nonviable pregnancy or a substantial threat to Sam's life, we would not entertain the thought of not welcoming our baby, no matter the complications.

Selecting through adoption, however, was another challenge altogether. Are we the best parents for a child with profound disabilities? We both have experience with working alongside disabled people, so maybe. But we are definitely not the best financially equipped family for raising a child with significant medical needs. We couldn't select for or against that possibility biologically, but would it be ethical or responsible to voluntarily *choose* a disabled child, knowing our material constraints and the challenges that generally face families accompanying disabled children? Our early forays into the world of adoption forms were a constant struggle to name what was *right* in our minds.

When we did become pregnant, we chose not to have screenings for Down syndrome, as we did not feel it would change anything about how we provided care for our child before their birth. I am not against scans and medicine, but I am against labeling a child too quickly and demanding that they fit immediately into a medicalized world, one that already dictates so much of our experience anyway. Still, without knowing, were we preventing ourselves from learning about likely supports they would one day need? Not every child with the same diagnosis needs the same supports, but still, we read childcare books not knowing what will really soothe our babies or how they'll take to breastfeeding, so what harm could more information do?

As we contended with the legal structures of the Scottish health-care system, in which genetic testing must always be offered and the date of conception becomes both a protection and liability, a significant question sat on us that remained constant regardless of the presence of a disability: How would our lives become different in the wake of this child coming to be?

No matter who they were, or what their specific needs would be, our lives would change. But how?

It is of course an impossible question. You simply cannot know. Maybe your baby is born with a rare heart defect that leads to years of surgeries and monitoring. Maybe they are born with cerebral palsy and you have years or decades of occupational therapy in your future. Maybe they have an intellectual disability and each year you will be forced to recount their failures in front of a board of teachers and administrators in order to receive some basic educational care. Or maybe they will lead their college basketball team to the Final Four. Who knows? In any case, what they do, what they need, and who they are will change your life as a parent. There's just no way to know if it is for the better or not.

ADOPTION

Considerations like these are what lead me to believe that all kids are, in some ways, adopted. A child is a totalizing system, one which changes us. Each one needs to be accepted, each needs to be cared for totally, not just in specific moments but all the time and always. There is a process of accepting them as part of the new whole. And that time is blurry. There were things we accepted right up front, like not having any guarantee that we were both fertile. There were things we began to accept during pregnancy, and then things we learned to accept once the kids arrived. Much like anyone we choose to become a caregiver for, children are wild cards. We may have a lot of assumptions and expectations, but we lack any certainty around who they will be, what they will need, and what it will require of us, and that scares a lot of people. Or maybe it scares everyone. Maybe some choose not to think about it, or only envision the possibilities that they deem positive. Maybe this is why genetic testing is so unquestioned and why gender reveals are so culturally resonant: if we at least know something about this kid, we can plan and prepare for our own futures a little more.

I think there is only one way to truly prepare for the changes a child brings, and it is to accept the responsibility and gift of accompanying this new life not without reservation but at least with an openness that says, "No matter who you are or become, no matter your needs, no matter your gifts and your struggles, I will go with you. I will be for you." As Ruth 1:16 says, "Where you go, I will go, and where you sleep, I will sleep. Your people shall be my people, and your God, my God."

It is far easier to entertain the idea of accompanying a baby, with absolutely no knowledge of whether they might have Down syndrome or a limb difference or something else, when the last decade of your life has been spent supporting your friends in assisted eating, interpreting augmentative and alternative communication technologies, and navigating Hoyer lifts. When worship has meant making communal music with your nonverbal friends and demanding pews get chopped in half to make space for wheelchairs. When you've seen God on display in people on the furthest edges of society's margins. When you have accompanied "those people," so much so that it has changed who you fundamentally are and has opened your eyes to the width and diversity of the God of the universe, it becomes easier to envision a world in which your baby is, at best, average, always needy, and not likely to win any type of national championship.

During our pregnancies, my desire was to protect our children from being claimed by that secular, medicalized, neoliberal approach which claims to tell us who each kid will be. This is the purpose of genetic testing: to define for the parents some future projection of their child, based on the assumption that "nondisabled" equals "normal." Instead, I wanted to keep them in the protective womb for as long as possible. Still, I have to concede that my kids were already "adopted" well before their due date. Our space was demarcated and altered. There is the room they will sleep in. It was the spare room; now it is theirs. This cabinet once held travel-sized toiletries, but now holds diaper cream and bath thermometers. That all happened, and well before they were here the altered space their presence demanded altered us.

This time of life, in which my world was being reshaped

in light of becoming a father, became increasingly poignant because of the timing of other major life events. Our first positive pregnancy test came the day after my father's funeral. We were actually out to pick up a test when we ran into two aunts and a former next-door neighbor, all shopping for Fourth of July festivities, including our annual family reunion. Sam had to shove the test into her purse and pray that the security cameras wouldn't think she was shoplifting.

After the funeral, and the reunion, we flew back to the UK. Our families didn't know; it was too early to tell people. But we knew. And it was impacting our conversations and plans already. We started looking for a bigger flat. And when parents started inquiring about visiting us in Aberdeen, we had to think about how pregnant Sam would be, and what limitations that would cause, even if we couldn't explain why those were considerations. Our child was already accompanying us in life, not just in taking up a small space inside Sam's womb but in reshaping what we could do, what we wanted, how we would live, and how we would spend our time.

If you have accepted the role of caregiving, you know these same constraints. "Can I go to dinner with my sister? Well, it depends on if my spouse is really agitated; dementia is so unpredictable." "Can I attend my high school reunion? I can trust my mom to correctly administer my kid's medicine that night, but if she's not free I don't think anyone else is a safe enough sitter." You plan around things, give up vacations and spontaneity, and get stuck in cycles where you don't know enough of the future to make plans with anyone but constantly wish people could be more involved in your life.

But because it is easier to see the caretaking of babies as a gift, I was able to start telling a new story about myself. Instead of being a boy who had just lost his father, I was becoming a father myself. English Romantic poet William Wordsworth, in his short verse "My Heart Leaps Up," named "the Child" as the "father of the Man," meaning that we must hold on to our childlike wonder at the world around us in a way that makes us who we are.[3] But in my case, it was a child to come, already a companion in many ways, that changed my self-understanding as no longer the end of a chain of men, but a link within it; a father, birthed by his child.

Following my father on his journey from active father to quadriplegic meant reconstructing his life's history to fit his new context. It was a long and arduous process, filled with emotional land mines and half-exposed traumas that, because he was changed but not gone, never felt fully open nor fully closed. It required each of us to find a new language to describe him, which ultimately came from a growing willingness to lean into the labels of disability. But as caregivers and family, we were excluded from this process of actualizing the new John who emerged after the accident. We had a different challenge: to become caregivers, adopting the new John and this radical new life spent moving at two miles per hour and taking thirty minutes to feed your own father a sandwich. A life in which we were restricted from certain spaces and gatherings, because we were tasked with keeping a disabled person safe even though we ourselves were not disabled.

Mélodie Kauffmann, a nurse and theology student, reflects on her experience of seeing family members deal with illness and disability, "The gut-wrenching powerlessness one feels while watching a loved one suffer from a long, painful, disabling disease is terrible. It can enrage you, even against the whole world."[4] Part of the struggle is that we understand, intimately if only partly, the change that is happening from "abled" to "disabled," but are cut out from the transition itself. Sure, there are some good resources for caregivers, spouses, children, and siblings, but ultimately we lack any accessible theological language that can renarrate our own lives in light of how we accompany someone else. That is why I've chosen to share this story; I want to help usher in a new vocabulary of accompaniment to our faith lives so that we can discover meaning in our situations, however diverse they may be, without using the lives of our loved ones as a means to our own ends. Instead, we can carry our histories along for the ride; we are enmeshed in the narratives around us, which our position as accompanists and caregivers brings to light. It is a gift to know that we are carrying a part of our disabled loved ones with us, because it reveals to us that other people must be carrying *us* as well. We can set down our independent streaks and acknowledge what is out of our hands. In doing so, we allow more space for God to show up in our lives.

Expanding our understanding of who is a caregiver, and what it means to accompany one another, helps all of us see the value of our past experiences. You don't need to have done disability ministry before having a child or had any special education before caring for a spouse after an accident. You have, assuredly, spent time with someone with open hands and a willingness to accept them for who they are—that can equip you to accompany others again in the future, or to see the way you currently support someone in a new light.

This is our baptismal promise. In entering into the kingdom of God and publicly confessing, we need not forsake our histories to be truly made anew in the Spirit. In our adoption into God's family, we are joined in our lives by the Christ who never forsakes us, no matter how many accommodations and supports we may need. Baptism is an announcement that we are choosing to live under God's authority and reliant on God's provision, whether we ace our LSAT or live on the streets or need walking sticks or have an extra chromosome. Our lives are not set by our genetics, or by how well we perform once we are part of God's kingdom, but by who has adopted us.

Each time we are privileged to worship by seeing someone be baptized, we renew our own baptism promise. In a baptism ritual, the congregation is tasked with following the baptized member as a newly adopted addition to the family. Working in college towns, which attract large numbers of highly mobile young people, it is abundantly clear that those who are baptized and raised in our church are unlikely to be the adults who shepherd the next generation. Rather, we walk alongside everyone who needs support, and accept care from all as well. "Remember your baptism" is the line that famously helped Luther ward off temptations, but in a more general sense it ought to encourage us to see God at work in us, through us, and with us at all times. Every moment, God is with us. When we profess that reality, alongside the community of God who witnesses it with us, we are taking an ongoing situation and highlighting it for just a moment. A beautiful, memorable moment, to be sure, but it only marks for a brief instance what is happening all the time and everywhere: God is Immanuel, with us.

Liturgy is God crafting us moment by moment. There are times of holiness and spaces that hold special weight, like a baptism, but really all times and spaces are weighty and holy because all times and spaces are used by God to produce us, right now. We do not worship God only on Sunday mornings in a stone building with fancy glass, but when each moment is offered to God for the renewing of the world. Everything we do is liturgy. Driving your car, stimming, reading to your spouse with dementia, walking a neighbor's dog, listening to a hyperfocused friend's monologue about Pokémon, fighting for your daughter's Individualized Education Program, shifting your father in bed to prevent bedsores—it's all the work of God's people, for God's people. Therefore it is all liturgy. All life is baptism and Communion, all space is church, all time is worship.

We remember our baptism when we accompany one another and when we acknowledge that we are accompanied by the Spirit. The history of God's redemption is being written into our bones as we speak, and it is our right and challenge as Christians to continuously celebrate our baptismal promises everywhere we go.

Ultimately, it is God alone who can fully renarrate our lives and redeem our histories. That is the promise of baptism, and it connects us with the transformative work of God throughout Scripture. Saul becomes Paul. David shifts from the runt of his large family to the king of Israel. Barren Sarai is transformed into Sarah the mother.

Mark 10 offers a short narrative in this same vein; Bartimaeus, who is blind, begs on the outskirts of Jericho. His name refers to his father, yet he sits as an outcast. Where is his family? Who is giving him care? Apparently, no one. His story is one of rejection, likely related to his disability. Yet, it is Bartimaeus who calls Jesus the Messiah in front of a large crowd, gathered in advance of the Passover when Jesus would be crucified. Bartimaeus is healed at the tail end of Jesus's ministry, and as the last healing miracle in the Gospel this chapter marks the transition from Jesus the preacher to Jesus the crucified and risen Savior. Bartimaeus himself is renarrated; he receives sight and therefore is thrust into a new relationship with his community, but crucially he does not magically transform from someone who is marginal to someone who is centered in the social scene. Rather, Jesus renarrates his experience of being outcast, and Bartimaeus finds liberation in following Jesus despite the transient and rough nature of walking mile after mile following a wandering preacher. Bartimaeus is still on the outskirts, but the outskirts of following Christ are filled with joy, love, grace, and wholeness.

WHO SHALL BE HEALED?

The healing narratives, in which a prophet or Christ physically changes someone's body, can be a difficult pill to swallow for many, of course. Biblical narratives often bear out the social experience of disabled people being weighed down with the expectations that they should want to change. Too often, we hold a false belief about what is normal, discounting the experiences of aging, accidents, disability, illness, even caregiving, and identifying them as aberrant. Reading about Jesus healing disabled bodies can reinforce this narrative if we aren't careful. But the world of the New Testament healing narratives is not the same as our world, and the way that Jesus heals cannot be viewed as the same thing as today's medical interventions. We need to read our Scriptures with this in mind, understanding that "healing" in the Bible is never just changing a body. As theologian Bethany Fox cautions us, "In our contemporary practices of healing, we need to pay attention to the symbolic world we inhabit and work within it to show how the kingdom of God is transforming what we think of as normal too."[5]

Why should the mute man in Matthew 9, the paralyzed man of John 5, or any other person healed in the Gospels need to have bodily changes in order to be part of the community? If they must be healed, what about those who are blind today? Or those who cannot walk? Are they condemned by omission? Is "faithfully disabled" an oxymoron?

Take, for instance, the stories of healing in Mark 5. First, Jesus encounters a man who is possessed, living in the tombs set in the wild space outside the city. Perhaps we can see this man still today, talking to himself on the street and sleeping in the minimal shelters of downtown doorways. He is seen as something to be subdued and controlled, and when he can't be, he is instead rejected from the safe space of the town. After exorcising the demons into a herd of pigs, Jesus leaves the man clothed and talking like all of the other townspeople. He is radically changed, made whole—or at least, made to be like the people of the town.

Following that, Jesus is approached by a woman who has been suffering from a bleeding issue, making her unclean and likely wildly uncomfortable. In her faith, she reaches out to touch just the hem of his robes, and she is proven correct. Her bleeding stops; her suffering ends. Jesus assures her, calming her fear with a pastoral word: "Daughter, your faith has made you well; go in peace and be cured of your disease."

In both stories, Christ exerts control over debilitating illnesses and mental health crises. So what about those who never see a break from their chronic illnesses and disabilities? What about those who are not healed? Are they lacking in the faith that healed the bleeding woman? This is often the challenge leveled at those seeking, but not finding, miraculous healing.

The burden weighing down disabled congregants from these "healing" texts can be heavy. It can be somewhat eased by acknowledging that Christ chose to heal only a select few, rather than all. To heal only *some* when one has the power to heal *all* means not claiming that illness or disability are completely wrong. Rather, it signifies healing as a symbol rather than the end goal. To heal, but in limited quantities, is to exercise authority over a body, which in turn gives us a major insight into the person of Jesus. The point is not to say that a blind body or a paralyzed body or a bleeding body is *wrong* and needs to be fixed, but instead to say that Christ has authority over all bodies of every sort.

I think this interpretation helps mitigate some of the more overt ableism found in much of Christian theology. These healing narratives can be used to claim that disabilities are outside of God's plan for the world, and this alternative perspective is more inclusive and welcoming (and, in my opinion, accurate). These biblical passages about healing can still be sticky, especially for people who earnestly desire to be healed but aren't. Preachers— and anyone attempting to apply biblical healing texts to people experiencing bodily struggles today—should think twice before doling out easy answers to those in the throes of disability, illness, or caregiving. Our world is rife with both ableism (the unreasonable privileging of able bodies) and disableism (the prejudice against disabled bodies), and it is foolish to think that we aren't impacted by that when we read our Bibles. These texts still hold authoritative meaning, of course, but only if we can apply them while attending to our own biases. That includes caregivers and care receivers alike; none of us are perfect, *including* disabled preachers like my great-uncle, Father Jim.

Jim was so dedicated a high school teacher that when he learned from his students about the realities of serving in Vietnam, he was so changed that he became an Army chaplain himself. He spent fourteen months in Korea before training as a paratrooper, completing eighty-three jumps. During his stint in Vietnam, Father Jim received multiple Bronze Stars for heroism under fire, all because as a teacher in southern Indiana, he was willing to let his life be changed by his students. What a model of accompaniment. Their new reality, having been re-created by their own trauma in war, gave him access to a new time, new place, new story, and it shaped the rest of his life. History has a funny way of repeating within families. Like me, Jim was ordained far from family while studying in Europe. And like my father, Jim was an avid bike rider until an accident led him to a life with quadriplegia. His religious leadership began early in life, and the years after his accident did little to change his sense of calling to ministry. He served in the Diocese of Evansville from late 1981 until his death, a span of forty years, and all from a seated position in his wheelchair. He spent twice as long in ministry as a quadriplegic than as an able-bodied man.

I wonder if he ever struggled to make sense of a story like Luke 5, in which a paralyzed man is lowered through a roof to bypass the crowds on his way to the feet of Jesus. Jim's own body, like my father's, fits narratively onto the unnamed man, but unlike in the Bible story, neither of these men was physically healed.

Were they held back by sin? Unbelief? A capricious and arbitrary God? Or, was healing offered elsewhere?

For a man who was willing to uproot his life and travel to Austria for years of study, and then to uproot again to live in the thick of war, maybe being among his close-knit family for his last several decades was the balm Jim needed. Maybe it was a source of frustration and anger. I do know that having a body that could run and cycle and skydive wasn't part of his baptismal calling. Maybe healing meant that he could be accompanied by his loved ones, rather than equipped to continue gallivanting across the globe. I don't know what his specific relationship with his disability was, nor should I assume anything. But I do know that he took a considerable amount of joy from spending time with his family and that his ministry was a source of light and love to a large community, and from my vantage point I can safely say that his life helped expand the kingdom. What a gift, to see that God is still at work and present even as the available world becomes smaller and smaller. The kingdom continues to expand, even as travel becomes inaccessible.

When James was baptized as an infant, his parents (my great-grandparents) promised to raise him within the church, living out a faithful commitment to God and God's people. Nowhere in the liturgy do parents promise the child that they will have an accident-free life. No baptismal covenant includes how many countries one may travel to. All that matters is that there is a public profession of God's authority over *this* life, *this* body.

Why are some people healed and not others? Why do some never experience much bodily degeneration their whole long lives, and others have physical pains and limits imposed from the start? Why do some men fall, break their spines, and live the rest of their days as quadriplegics, and others do not?

I don't know. I suspect those who suffer these pains and accidents did not know, either. But I also know that a theology of accompaniment requires that we be so attentive to the lives of others that we can be shaped by their experiences ourselves; not that I have lived life as a quadriplegic, but I have been marked by a history that cannot be separated from these men. Most importantly, each one of us is accompanied by the Spirit, always giving us access to the kingdom of God made present among ourselves without requiring our bodies to look, feel, or move any certain way. Indeed, Father Jim's ministry was no less rich and meaningful after his accident, not because his body was marked by his accident but because God's power could be displayed in a new way that widened our understanding of what it means to live out our baptisms. This is what it means to proclaim the Good News with our whole lives. This also means that our lives are meant to showcase God's presence regardless of our circumstance.

In John 9:1–41 and again in John 11:1–44, Jesus displays a significant power over bodies: first, by healing a man who was born blind, and later, by raising Lazarus from the dead. In both stories, Jesus announces that these works are done so that God might be glorified. At first blush, this might imply that it is God who has blinded this man, and God who has killed Lazarus. If that were the case, though, Jesus would be effectively undoing God's work. Rather, the better way to understand these stories is that disabilities and death happen. They simply exist. Putting our boundaries too narrow, however, and creating a theological system in which disability and death only exist outside of the goodness of God, limits where we can see God at work. Then, we only see the miracle if the blind man sees or the dead man is raised to new life. But all of life is an opportunity for God's presence to be made known. God can be displayed in a new way, through the life of a blind beggar on the street, in the weeping of sisters over the body of their brother, and in the world-traveling hotshot teacher staying home to foster decades of deep ministry. This is a broader understanding of healing, less focused on a cure for medically broken bodies and more in tune with the Spirit's work within each person, whether they fit inside our limited boundaries or not.

Going through life with a nondisabled father who suddenly becomes very visibly disabled is jarring. But the history we carry with us can help us understand where we find ourselves now. I grew up with no knowledge of Father Jim the paratrooping competitive cyclist. Instead, I only knew Father Jim the priest who used an electric wheelchair and had modifications in his apartment so he could live independently. When my father became disabled, and I suddenly entered a position of accompanying him through this new phase, my perception of our family history emerged as a key foundation for my new role.

But also, my understanding of the healing narratives in the Bible helped create my new sense of self. For nearly every person healed, there are named and purposefully unnamed accompanists nearby. Families, both supportive (Simon Peter, supporting his feverish and ailing mother-in-law in Luke 4) and dismissive (a blind man's parents, sending the suspicious authorities to their healed son instead of supporting him in John 9); friends who are dedicated enough to commit pretty significant property damage (lowering a paralyzed man through a roof in Mark 2); people conspicuously missing from someone's life, so much that no one is there to lower him into a healing pool (John 5)— all of these are stories that feature the potential power of being a dedicated caregiver, and highlight the challenge for disabled people who lack those safety nets.

Together, my family history and my religious upbringing wove a new narrative that I could tell for myself. This one was bound by my experience of emptying catheter bags and locking wheelchairs into vans, but written for me by God.

Trauma at UT

While I remember almost nothing about my stay at the University of Tennessee Trauma Center (UT), my family reported to me that we had several sensible conversations about the accident and my condition. Unfortunately, Cherry held the burden of interacting with medical personnel and making decisions about my care—a heavy load for her, and frustrating for the ways she was too often dismissed by medical professionals.

She and my two oldest children, Emily and Michael, arrived at the trauma center about two or three in the morning. Because Topher was hiking with me when I tripped, he was the first to reach the hospital. By the time Cherry and the other kids arrived, he had still not received any information nor seen a doctor. Not only would the staff not let any of them see me, they were also tight-lipped about my condition.

After their arrival, but before they could see me, Terry, the overnight nurse, wanted my medical history from Cherry and ignored all of her questions about my status. Despite not being remotely qualified to make such a pronouncement, nor structurally charged with delivering such news, nurse Terry then said she wasn't worried about getting things like an MRI scheduled quickly because with high-level spinal cord injuries, "What you see is what you get."

Nurse Terry continued to ask them stupid questions, as if it mattered at that moment whether I was up-to-date on my flu shots. Cherry later filed a formal complaint against nurse Terry for overstepping her role and for her blatant insensitivity and was told that there would be a review. A minor victory, frankly.

Doctors finally came into the waiting room to collect the family, well over thirty minutes after their arrival and still without Michael and Topher having seen me at all. They announced that I was to have surgery—at first, imminently, and later, pushed back a day. There was really no way to ever know when things would happen. Maybe the hospital staff didn't know themselves. They certainly didn't share much with us.

Once it was determined that I would have surgery, Cherry contacted my brother Thom, who rallied all my siblings to head to Knoxville. The surgery that Monday went well and the surgeon gave a very positive report: no damage to my spinal cord. The problem was caused by my third vertebra slamming into the fourth, causing the cord to kink. His assessment was that I would enjoy a complete recovery once the considerable amount of swelling went down. Upon hearing this news, and on the heels of a very stress-filled past few days, the family celebrated over a nice dinner with wine.

The news spread quickly and my family's phones were swamped with calls and text messages. Responding to all of these calls proved impossible, which is ostensibly one of the few good problems in the midst of a spinal cord injury situation. Emily employed her experience as an English teacher to set up a CaringBridge website, which allowed everyone in my family to share brief updates with anyone interested. Over the nine months of my treatment, the site received over fifty-five thousand visits from family, friends, and colleagues.

Meanwhile, Topher came up with a letter board that we could use for me to communicate postsurgery. Without getting overly graphic, the best access point for my injured spinal cord was through the front of my neck, which meant I would not be able to speak while I recovered from surgery. Using the board was helpful, but laborious and filled with errors.

A day or two after the surgery I asked to "talk" with my uncle, Father Jim. Jim is a Catholic priest and retired US Army chaplain. He is also a quadriplegic, initially injured during a rappelling training exercise accident and further compounded by a bicycle crash. These two incidents had occurred about one week apart nearly thirty years before. Though Father Jim is also a quadriplegic, there are several critical differences between our injuries and functionalities.

There is a whole spectrum of spinal cord injuries. Spinal cord injuries are classified by the highest vertebra affected. From top to bottom, the spinal cord is divided into five areas: cervical, thoracic, lumbar, sacral, and coccygeal. The nerves branching off of the spinal cord roughly correspond to body parts from top to bottom when sitting. The cervical area connects to the head and shoulders while the lumbar connects to the legs. As a general rule, the higher the level of injury, the more profound the level of paralysis. Of course, every human body is different and the medical models don't necessarily align with every person.

A serious concern for those who incur injuries to the fifth cervical vertebra or higher is the effect on the respiratory system. Such injuries often cause paralysis of the diaphragm and may require reliance on a ventilator. Later, we came to believe that my diaphragm had indeed been slightly paralyzed in my accident, which complicated my transition away from using a ventilator.

The World Health Organization (WHO) estimates that 15.4 million people globally are living with a spinal cord injury.[6] In the United States, the largest number of these injuries come from car accidents, although about a quarter come from falls, like mine. Around a third of all people with spinal cord injuries are classified as "neurologically incomplete quadriplegic," which means that a person may have less functional use of their hands, back, and legs, but retain some movement. Most can use a manual wheelchair without assistance and many are able to drive. For the most part, they lead independent lives. This describes both Father Jim and Shane, the professor who shared my story without my (or Topher's) permission, as he used me to illustrate the diversity of spinal cord injuries (SCIs).

Around 17 to 18 percent of us have neurologically complete quadriplegia. I usually say "complete quad," which seems to help people understand better what my function is and isn't. Most in my category are paralyzed from the neck down, while a few have paralysis above the neck as well. All quadriplegics require an extreme amount of help with activities that are routine for most people. Most complete quadriplegics need assistance with the activities of daily living, including eating, bathing, dressing, and toileting. In addition, help is often required for other activities, such as writing, reading, coughing, sleeping, changing TV channels, and making phone calls. In addition, between 3.4 and 6 percent of quadriplegics breathe with assistance from a ventilator.[7]

Initially, I was put on a ventilator full-time. Being connected to a ventilator prevented me from talking normally, and would have prevented me from going anywhere without bringing a portable ventilator. This would have significantly lowered my quality of life and is associated with a massive jump in mortality rates. As a result, a lot of my therapy was aimed at restoring my capacity to breathe unassisted.

Vent-dependent patients have two common ways of communicating. One is to insert a speaking valve into the trachea. I initially had no luck with using a speaking valve, so I was left with the tedious method of using the character board to communicate. People would point to the different rows of letters and numbers, and when they got to the row containing the desired character, I would nod my head. They would then run the pointer down the row until they reached the desired character.

The board was incredibly difficult to use, and it took considerable effort to communicate my desire to talk with Father Jim. I tried spelling "F R J" only to be stopped and told this was nonsense. I finally was able to get Jim on the phone, though I don't remember most of the call, and I was told that our conversation was short. He suggested that my injury was much more extensive than his, which greatly disheartened my family and lowered their perspective on my prospects for recovery.

My oldest brother, Dick, had remained in Chicago to prepare for our presumed arrival, while my other siblings, Thom, Steve, and Janet, were beside themselves. Cherry got up every day, dressed and applied makeup as if she was going to work, and came to the hospital. The rest of the family took turns visiting me in the intensive care unit. As I was quite anxious and confused, Cherry insisted that no one cry in my presence. I was strapped on a board and could only see in one direction. Cherry put the kids and my siblings on a rotation around this board such that I could never see a visitor's immediate reaction to my situation. While none of this was necessary, it was of primary concern to her that my spirits might remain higher than the tension around me.

The twelve days following the surgery were spent trying to keep me alive. Spinal cord injuries are so complex, given that they link every part of your body. The physical shock to the body takes a toll on every system, internal and external. Plus, pneumonia had set in. I needed to be transferred to a qualified rehabilitation facility. The first option was a lower-level rehab center in our hometown. Cherry and the family insisted that a major rehabilitation center was the correct place for me instead, but they had to find one. My sister, a physician from Pittsburgh, promoted the idea of me going to the University of Pittsburgh Medical Center. Topher actively researched rehabilitation facilities and argued for me to go instead to the Rehabilitation Institute of Chicago (RIC).

He zeroed in on RIC because it was considered one of the premier rehab facilities in the United States. It was also close to where my brother Dick lived, which meant Cherry could stay with family during my stay. But two problems prohibited the move. First, RIC was full. Second, the family was first told that RIC did not take patients who were on a ventilator (which we later found to be false, but the complexity of information and medical needs regularly led to significant misunderstandings like this).

After some further searching, the family found another facility in the Chicago suburbs, which I'll call 'AFP.' We thought this place could assist me in recovery, especially weaning off of my vent so that I could qualify for RIC when a bed opened. The proximity to the home of Dick and his wife, Josie, was icing on the cake.

Interestingly, while I was not involved in any of these conversations, some details of them crept into my subconscious. I had many dreams and nightmares throughout my rehabilitation time, and I vividly remember one in which I had the choice of going to RIC or to a treatment center in Pittsburgh. Dream-RIC rehabbed individuals with the goal of returning to normal society, but they would retain some level of paralysis. The Pittsburgh center offered a complete recovery, but only if the person made the choice to live permanently underwater.

While at UT, my health continued to decline rapidly, so much so that Cherry and others believed that I would not live if I stayed in Tennessee much longer. A decision had to be made, and at that moment AFP was the only viable choice. Plans got under way to move me from Knoxville to Chicago via air transport.

In the midst of preparations to be moved, I developed a fever. UT refused to release me with a fever and AFP refused to accept me with a fever. Michael, a problem solver at heart, kicked family members out of my room and, in cahoots with a nurse, located a large amount of ice. The nurse provided a lot of extra large plastic bags and towels. Michael covered me in ice all night long, such that when rounds were performed in the morning my temperature was normal.

The move was back on. Unfortunately, Mike's fever remedy didn't last, and in the airplane hangar my fever returned. At that point, neither UT nor AFP wanted me.

5

Space

What Can We Access?

Everywhere I go, I try to fit in a run. I love marking where I've been, so I offer up my personal data as a sacrifice to the technology company overlords (who probably already have it anyway) and GPS-track myself as I dart in and out of traffic all through various cities of the world. It also helps me see parts of cities that are typically beyond the traditional realm of tourists. The parts that aren't filled with the cool coffee shops and trendy art houses, or famous historic buildings and important statues, or iconic art museums and whatnot.

I start my watch, take off, maybe pause to snap a few pics of cool graffiti, and my feet leave a virtual blue line around the city streets, viewable on my computer whenever I want to remember how cool the backstreets of Brussels are or how surprisingly tranquil Stockholm can be.

Having lived in Nashville, then Austin, places that attract a lot of tourists (often for concerts or bachelorette parties), I know that visiting a city is not the same as living there. Spending four days in Amsterdam in no way teaches me what it is like to live in Amsterdam. So when I travel, I run. Sometimes I run to places that the runners in the city might go to, major parks and big boulevards with wide sidewalks and the like. Usually, though, I find backstreets and canals, looping over to cover a wide cross section of the city.

My running maps tell a different story than my photos. The alley that features piles of rubbish and the stale scent of urine (dog? no, definitely human) gets the same blue line as the round-about at the Arc de Triomphe. One line is not bigger or brighter just because tourists stop to take photos of one more than the other. My photos, however, show off the museums and my standard breakfast of a croissant and expresso.[1] Cities change depending on how we choose to map them. If I show you my running routes, I show you one city. If I show you my curated photos, you see a totally different place.

And sometimes, neither photos nor maps can show you the reality of experiencing a city. In Amsterdam, I had to constantly stop for traffic because the sidewalk ran out without warning, but my running map shows an unimpeded loop weaving across the canals. My photos mostly show a lovely boat tour and the quirky, leaning buildings instead of me grumbling about the irrationality of a city filled with both canals and cars.

To be able to run up and down these streets relied on me having lungs and a heart and muscles that were strong enough to carry my weight, which, as an asthmatic, I can never take for granted. But it also relied on me having access. In Paris and Amsterdam, access came from the privilege of being a tourist. In midtown Nashville, I was able to live and run partly by living in a co-op of ministry students whose building was grandfathered in for affordable property taxes. (I could not have afforded to live next door to Taylor Swift's penthouse apartment otherwise!)

Beyond the physical needs for running and the economic access to that neighborhood, I look a certain way. I am white and male and was young enough to not need to worry about being accosted in the street. I had decent running shoes, and "proper" athletic gear; the bright neons signified to the people around me that I was not running for some nefarious purpose but was engaging in something reputable like physical exercise. Runners love to talk about how cheap it is to run—all you need is some supportive shoes, and you are out the door! But of course, that's the privilege of being white and having the benefit of doubt. If I were older, nonmale, nonwhite, these things may have been off-limits to me, no matter how bright my shoes or short my shorts.

The world is in many ways a beautiful place filled with incredible experiences and wonderful people. It is also sometimes a bag of crap. For me, it is often a lot easier to find the wonderful bits because very few people are actively trying to prevent me from living a full and abundant life. But the realization that I can enjoy certain things while others simply cannot helps me to also see that the beautiful bits of life can't really be enjoyed when the mundane bits are broken.

Austin isn't quite so fun when you realize the stark economic differences between zip codes. Nashville is kind of a downer when you think about the disproportionate police practices in communities of color. Aberdeen loses some sparkle when it confronts you with its sex trafficking problem. So what do we do? Do we only focus on the nice sections? Live in sight of the Top Ten things to see, so that we're always surrounded by the best and brightest and least confrontational aspects of where we live? Or do we run through the alleys, dodging puddles of urine, and work to help those whose experiences diverge unfairly from our own?

If we are to be salt and light in this world, it will challenge us to not just see our spaces with new eyes. It will go beyond that. It will force us to accompany our places, just as we journey with one another.

TRAVEL

Postaccident, my father attended functions with a tenuous dignity, alert but unable to brace for the slightest malfunction, a spasm, a leaky catheter, that would betray his abled mind to the indignity of infancy, the resigned Stoic becoming the living prop for well-intentioned and disdained necessities. To be beholden to the muscles and dexterity of others, particularly one's own children, as they feed, change, and wipe you is a painful reminder of the expected years taken. His hands ought to have shaken mine after at least one graduation, and held at least one grandchild, and gripped his bicycle handles for at least one more overly lengthy sojourn. He had time. His body was healthy in all the conventional ways doctors seem to want fifty-six-year-old bodies to be, so that they can exercise, play with their grandchildren, and offer a still-strong grip when they acknowledge the years of hard mental work by their kid in robe and mortarboard. But he did not do these things.

He could not travel to any of my graduations. The first, my undergrad from Purdue, was prohibited by a complete lack of resources and physical capacity. At the time, he was still residing in Chicago, with his days spent at rehab doing the physical work of learning to breathe, chew, swallow, and talk. My mother commuted between my aunt and uncle in a western suburb and a downtown hotel room two blocks from the hospital.

Just before St. Patrick's Day, not long before I finished my degree, he was allowed to try his new powered wheelchair outside for the first time. He and I navigated to the lobby, under a thirty-foot tapestry of Job 14:7 (KJV), "For there is hope of a tree, if it be cut down, that it will sprout again, and that the tender branch thereof will not cease," and into the chilly Chicago downtown.

We walked and rolled with relative ease to the Chicago River, where green dye had been added hours before. In the waning twilight, we could just make out the vibrant color.

There is a photo of this moment, taken by a stranger. In a strange sense, it made the experience shockingly normal. A boy and his dad out for a walk, eager to see the kitschy holiday decor in the big city. Two men, bundled and talking in fits and starts between ever-flowing foot traffic and stoplights. Just two people going somewhere together. Normal.

But this was his very first time using the chair in the real world. He had only done a few laps down the smooth hallways of a rehab hospital before this, yet he had the confidence of a pro athlete in a pickup game. When we eventually returned, a nurse scolded him, because, unbeknownst to me, his charge had been to take the chair once around the block and return, and go no farther. They had been waiting for an hour, assuming the worst.

On our return from the verdant river, we cut through a building, hoping to find an elevator and shortcut. Whole books have been written about the unique wayfinding of wheelchair users. Elizabeth Guffey traced the unique culture that comes along with the secret routes that chairs take you. Certain paths that were never noticed become the only way forward, and while modern signage is helpful, the existence of such symbols is a misfit, meant for misfits, demarcating "separate but equal" access in a world predicated on both equality and rampant physical ableism.[2]

In this downtown high-rise, we were beginning to find that a chair was a radically different way of moving through the world, a way not always welcomed by architecture or the glances of strangers. In Chicago, because of the lake and the northern latitude, many downtown buildings utilize a mechanized set of double doors, in which the outer door must shut before the inner door can open. This is, to my limited knowledge, only true for power-assisted doors, the kind operated by buttons. Now, this does have the effect of keeping some minimal amount of cold air out, and that is a fair perk. But also, it is quite difficult to navigate crowded Chicago entry spaces when the doors you need to open are smashing into a chair and you can't back up because only one door opens at a time and you can't turn right because the manual door is being held open for folks walking through and you get so jammed that the only way out is to run over your son's foot with several hundred pounds of wheeled force.

This chair, which opened many possibilities, could only be transported by a special van, one which we did not yet have. So, although I graduated from his alma mater, a place he'd visited countless times for football tailgates, family weekends, and my sister's and brother's graduations, he did not attend mine. He simply could not.

That summer, he finally returned home. His homecoming and my graduation were celebrated together. We set out a cake for me, while he was justifiably the focal point. In preparation to bring him home, we built ramps in the garage for him to get into the house and had an extension built onto the back corner of our house. Just behind the laundry room, with a separate ramped entrance, was his new room, complete with an accessible bathroom and wheel-in shower. Had we not had professional builders on both sides of my family, as well as volunteers from our church, I doubt this suite would have been possible. And had he not been able to retreat to this safe room, built specifically with his chair and needs in mind, no such celebration could have gathered.

My second graduation, this time in Nashville, which is an hour and a half closer to our hometown than Purdue, was disrupted less by his physical or technological constraints and more so by a failure of imagination. Although he could conceivably sit in a car long enough to travel out of state, he would have needed a specialty room to stay in, far beyond what a typical ADA-compliant hotel offers. He would not have been able to readily access the outdoor graduation grounds if it had rained prior, as his wheels would have been too heavy to navigate muddy turf. Our school, despite priding itself on inclusion, diversity, and justice, had no ramps available between the multiple celebration spaces. Later, when I got married in Nashville, we broached all of these same issues again. A very generous friend and classmate of mine, now a nurse practitioner, helped me research short-term hospital bed rentals and voluntary hospital stays. She even offered to act as his personal caregiver for the big day, accompanying him through catheter changes, pressure breaks, and assisted feeding while forgoing the experience of attending a wedding with a group of her friends. She was generous to offer, but a van, a bed, and an attendant were not the only barriers.

By then, my father had become so accustomed to his room that the comfort it offered became a source of security. Too often denied access and forced to bounce painfully over barriers that ought to have been smoothed, his body and mind together drew inward to spaces that did not assault his senses. Can I really fault him for being restrictive about where he was willing to go, where he would eat, what roads he would travel on? Would you want to navigate a city, and world, that didn't plan for your body? While he ultimately did attend my wedding, he left early to drive back across two states and be safe in his own bed.

He did not attend my third graduation because he did not have proper travel documents to enter Scotland, and it was restricted for COVID, and because he was dead.

As I shared in chapter 2, the temporal disruption of a life trajectory often causes grief. Consider the pain experienced by an adult who needs one's aging parents to diaper and feed them once again, familiar caregiving made strange by the unexpected timing and role-switching. Parents are meant to die before children; we are kept clean and fed by them until we are self-sufficient, and then we take the role of caring for their degenerating bodies before death; it is the rhythm of life.

This disruption is not restricted to the temporal, but also shifts (often in unwelcome ways) how we engage the space around us. Living in a disrupted time means living in a disrupted spatial world. A friend undergoing chemotherapy mentioned how work travel became a privilege that she could no longer afford, as being available at the hospital for treatments quickly became the center of both her time and her space. She couldn't afford to go too far away in case she got stuck, missing her next treatment. Her future needs shaped how and where she could inhabit the present.

Of course, the disruption of the expected timeline can cause grief, too. Not having one's father at a graduation is a moment of grief. The failure of the expected timeline is heightened by the ways space itself seems to fracture when the people you've journeyed with are no longer present. Maybe it was naive to think that our closest people would always be with us, whether family or friends. But even if there is a logic in knowing that people drift apart, accidents happen, and death comes at uneven intervals, the grief persists.

Some spaces may be permanently marred by that grief.

And yet . . .

Even in the hardest of situations, when all seems lost and broken, the Spirit helps us create new things. We are never left on our own, no matter how the losses mount. Theology isn't always the most comforting of practices. The arcane words, the technicalities, the challenge of blending academic philosophy, ethics, and history—it all adds up to something that too often feels foreign and confusing. But T. F. Torrance, a Scottish theologian, offered a deeply insightful understanding of a theology of space that can serve not just as a challenging exercise for our minds, but also as hope for our souls.

We often think of space as the places we inhabit. Maybe like a giant grid that stuff can drop onto, like the world is a chessboard and our roads, buildings, trees, yards, and selves are all just the game pieces. In that view, God is just the board. But Torrance offers some intriguing counters for us to imagine. Rather than think about God as the board on which we stand, we ought to acknowledge that the very concepts of space and time are simply creations themselves, all existing within the location of Jesus Christ, God incarnate, "where God meets with man in the actualities of human existence, and man meets with God and knows him in His own divine Being."[3]

In other words, space is contained within God rather than God enclosed within space. Only through Jesus Christ, who is both transcendent and incarnate, can any of us find room for the Divine. Sometimes, people like to use the language of "inviting Jesus into our hearts." But we aren't receptacles for God. Instead, Jesus is God, fully, which means that space itself is his body. And, despite the oddity of how theology is argued, that gives me a deep comfort.

Jesus is the body that forms space itself, and so even in the most crushing of griefs we are met by the One who restores us and offers us respite. Anywhere and everywhere we go, no matter if our personal histories have broken a specific place for us or our narratives have wounded a given time, we are confronted with the reality that our time, narratives, space, histories, and performances are not fully ours. They belong to Christ. They belong to the people around us. And we are offered a respite, a healing, a restoration, to the ways each perspective is broken.

Hospital rooms can be awful. Weird lighting, strange smells, lots of scary-looking equipment, and a steady stream of doctors and nurses invading your privacy. Even worse, the room represents a medical need, some pain in the body that requires intervention. No matter how nice, airy, and clean the hospital tries to make them, no one wants to be in there.

What if, though, that hospital room is in fact formed from the body of Christ? What if, when we accompany our loved one into that medical building, we are already immersed in our Savior? What if we knew that Jesus was present, even amid the beeping machines and intravenous drips and bedpans? Maybe, if we head into that space with the acknowledgment that even there, the body of Christ is all around us, it might not be so scary. Or, at least we can take our fears to God that much more readily.

What does your caregiving space look like? What does it *feel* like? Do you feel trapped? Claustrophobic? Like the spaces where you spend your time don't have enough room for you to feed someone else and still breathe for yourself? Maybe the room your loved one uses most often, a bedroom or a living room, feels oppressive, like there is a specter looming, demanding your time and attention constantly. If so, does the rest of the house feel cold and empty, or does it feel like a small oasis, a space where you can avoid the responsibilities of spoon-feeding someone cereal, stretching spastic muscles every morning, repositioning the person every two hours, constantly moving their lift and bedside table around so they can see their TV, and scratching their nose for them? Has your bedroom transformed from a place of safety and comfort, shared with a spouse, into a place that no longer feels like it belongs to you? Has your TV transformed from a few shows a week to constant background noise to keep someone else company? The valued mementos of travels and special occasions overtaken by medical equipment and pill organizers? Without downplaying the heartache this spatial shift can cause, we must also acknowledge the possibility that God is still every bit as active in the places that no longer feel like *life*. Jesus is there, as your aging mother refuses to move the table she has tripped on three times. The Spirit is hovering, as your husband with dementia looks at your wedding photo on your mantel and asks, "Who are those people?" God dwells with you, as your child vomits on their bedsheets throughout the night after a rough dose of chemotherapy.

Even the empty space where someone used to sit, and never will again, is a space constituted by the body of Christ. It can be redeemed. The time we have lost to accidents and illness is constituted by Jesus; it, too, can be redeemed. Our stories, our histories, and our performances, all of these are rooted fundamentally in the person of Christ. All can be redeemed, because in them the Spirit accompanies us.

Good theology, no matter how confusing and philosophical, should always point back to the reality of God's love for us and the ever-present hope that all things, all times, all stories, and all spaces, can be redeemed.

JOHN'S STORY, PART 5

Chicago

My care plan called for me to be moved to the site I'll call AFP in the Chicago suburbs. This move addressed two issues: first, it was a place to receive care while I was awaiting a room at the Rehabilitation Institute of Chicago (RIC). Second, AFP's specialty was treating respiratory issues, a major problem for me at this point.

While people tell me that I was cognizant from time to time in the trauma center, it was while lying in the airplane that I briefly returned to full consciousness and my memories became somewhat cohesive. Cherry joined me and the airborne EMT on the flight to Chicago. With the three of us and the necessary medical equipment, the space in the small twin-engine plane was extremely cramped. This was going to be the least of our worries.

At some point during the flight the door adjacent to my gurney came loose. With the broken seal came strong gusts of cold air and extremely loud noises. While we know in retrospect that there was no danger of a door failure, at the time I was very afraid that the door was going to come off completely. No sooner did the door get fixed than another problem arose. Specifically, we were informed by the medical attendant that there was a chance I would run out of oxygen before we arrived in Chicago. This poor planning had created a problem that made the tight quarters and loose door pale in comparison.

Because my medical status was tenuous at best, these flight issues were a matter of life and death. About the time we landed in Chicago, I lost consciousness again. I have no memory of the ride to AFP out in the western suburbs of Chicagoland.

Due to being unconscious for so much of each day, my memories of the stay at AFP are sporadic and disconnected. My family filled in many gaps for me, often using frustrated tones and colorful language. Despite my haze, I felt strongly that the operations at AFP were compartmentalized to a fault and communications were poor, often resulting in careless care. At times, I even felt that the medical treatment was dangerous.[4]

At one point, Topher mentioned to me that he was considering preemptively quitting the divinity graduate program he had just been accepted to in favor of pursuing a master of hospital administration. He figured if this hospital was highly regarded and functioned so poorly, he couldn't possibly do worse. I think he was joking, but my brother later mentioned it might be a good career move for him, so clearly it was a discussion beyond just my bedside.

Terrible leg spasms afflicted me constantly. Since I had no primary doctor assigned specifically to me, I inquired of one of the rotating physicians about treatment to reduce the spasms. His response was, "I'll let somebody else take care of that." Apparently no referral was ever made, because the situation was never addressed.

Weaning me off of the ventilator was the number one priority of my time at AFP. Doing so would set the stage for my long-term prognosis, determining my ability to eat normally and to live life untethered. However, during the whole weaning process I had lots of very unsettling experiences. Ultimately the process was unsuccessful at AFP, although I would eventually learn to breathe on my own.

The weaning process made no sense to me. The basic practice was to remove access to oxygen and force me to breathe on my own for a predetermined length of time. Once I was successful, the length of time without oxygen would be increased. The incremental increases were large and I was expected to tell the therapist when I needed to return to the oxygen. I knew that being free from the ventilator was critical to the possibility of a normal life. The therapists' frequent admonitions that I would be tethered to a ventilator for life if I failed in the weaning process seemed like a threat to me. As a result I developed a strong fear of a lifetime dependency upon a machine. Consequently, I sometimes waited too long to ask for help. During these periods, the resultant lack of oxygen would make everything seem surreal. Often I awoke feeling like I was hanging upside down in total darkness. I was tied up and could not open my mouth. I never knew where I was. Once, I recall watching a football game with players running perpendicular to the wall, off the screen. Life without oxygen made no sense.

AFP employed one respiratory therapist I'll call Chuck who could best be described as a classic showboat. He thought that by using his superior skills I could be weaned from my respirator much faster than was called for in my care plan. During one particular treatment, Chuck, against any reasonable medical standard, turned down the oxygen rate on my respirator so low that my O2 dropped to a dangerous level. It took several doctors quite a while to bring my oxygen rate back into a safe range.

Even though Chuck was a risky daredevil and a danger, he remained in the respiratory therapist pool. Whenever his number was called to care for me, even though I could only mouth words, I would look at Cherry and say, "Fuck Chuck!"

In addition to the inadequate medical treatment, especially at night, AFP produced multiple stresses. I was totally immobile and at great risk of developing wounds. Patient aides were required to turn me on a strict two-hour schedule. To say that the aides were inattentive and obnoxious is an understatement. It was normal for them to tend to me while carrying on boisterous, unrelated personal conversations and throw my body around. At that point I could not speak and had no recourse. AFP was also undergoing a building renovation. The majority of this work was conducted at night, and this was just one more thing that made sleep extremely difficult.

One side effect of using a respirator is that I could not get rid of normal throat secretions and discharge by coughing, spitting, or swallowing. My secretions were significantly greater because of the trauma. To collect these secretions a suction tube would be forced down my throat. Depending upon the amount of the secretions this procedure would be performed between ten and thirty times each day. Early on, this procedure was quite distressing because it triggered the natural gag response. After a while, however, it became a routine part of my daily regimen. Well, "routine" may not be the right word because there were still occasional problems, and some of them were quite dangerous.

I had multiple bad experiences with medical staff that I'll never forget. One nurse in particular would often ignore my care preferences. One evening I was extremely restless and in some amount of pain. She offered me a particular medicine to calm me down and reduce the discomfort. Unfortunately, I had experienced negative effects of the drug she was offering, so I was adamant in refusing it. Totally ignoring me, she proceeded to slip it in with my nightly medications. It was only after the side effects became apparent that I realized what she had done. Once again, because I was not able to speak, I could not address the issue directly.

By this time, I had changed dramatically. I looked twenty years older and was suffering from insomnia. One morning I reported to Cherry that the nurse thought that I just needed to sleep and didn't need assistance in doing so. She refused to give me a sleeping aid, and I suffered through a very restless night. Cherry spoke with the nurse and it was agreed that I would be given the drug upon request. After the second night of restlessness, Cherry confronted the nurse directly regarding her unwillingness to administer a drug that was clearly identified in my chart. After one more night without this sleeping aid, Cherry relayed the story to another nurse who, as it happened, was the supervisor. She confirmed that my nurse had been instructed to provide the drug. "Nurse Ratched," as Cherry and I deemed her, was summarily dismissed from attending to me and I never saw her again.

In general, AFP was a terrible experience. They failed in their efforts to wean me off the respirator, they failed to stabilize my condition in general, they failed to have a coherent plan of treatment, and they failed to communicate with me or with my family. To this day, my family carps about not being kept abreast of my needs, medical treatment plans, and the expected prognosis.

I turned fifty-six years old at AFP on November 7, 2010. Cherry told me that I was so exhausted from the attempts at weaning and other rehabilitation activities that I had little desire to visit with friends and family other than my wife, brother, and children. She covered for me, and we did ultimately celebrate with visits from select family members. Interactions with large groups of people presented a challenge, and while we were grateful for their efforts, it was just too much at times.

For a month following my birthday, I continued to work on my diaphragm strength and my ability to breathe without additional oxygen. In what might be deemed a "Thanksgiving miracle," I was given the chance to escape AFP and find a rehab center more capable of handling my complex needs. Without the advocacy, and frustrations, of my family, I likely would never have made it out alive.

6

Performance

Living Into Our Vocation as God's Children

My father was not what you would call a performer. Sure, he could command a room if necessary, and he was gregarious and outgoing and sociable, so it would seem like he was a performer at times. And sure, he was no stranger to being the biggest personality in a group, and when you combine that with a sense of confidence, you tend to get performances. But he was, for the most part, not a performer.

Parents become performers. It's part of the job, adopting voices and backstories for otherwise nameless toys, feigning etiquette for invisible tea parties, and grimacing through the early stages of a youngling learning a new instrument. Play is important. I learned to "box" my dad when I was barely walking. He loved to teach everyone how to shadowbox, how to bounce on the balls of your feet, keep the wrists loose, and throw a punch out, landing not against flesh but close enough that the wind would fling into the eyes of the brave (or unsuspecting) recipient. Sometimes, parents don't feel like playing along. The toy telephone rings, and you want to let it go to voice mail. But you pick it up anyway, because you know it means the actual world to a two-year-old.

My dad was keen to play things, but would never be described as playful. He was apt and quick to engage, bold and confident, yet never a performer.

When my niece, Ruth, was born, that changed. The man who taught me things like motion paradoxes at the dinner table when I was ten became a grandfather, so discussions of quantum mechanics and the ecology of strip mining gave way to songs again. He was clearly out of practice, given that his youngest was twenty-nine years old by then, and I was ever eager to give up those "infantile" pursuits as soon as I could.

Ruth made my dad sing again, for the first time in decades.

I don't know if he really enjoyed it or not. But he had the self-confidence to sing to a baby, not in the hidden safety of a quiet nursery where no one else can hear or judge you, but in full earshot of whoever was holding his granddaughter on his behalf. People would hold Ruth up near his chest when she was small and immobile, and as she grew, would create opportunities that approximated play. If Ruth was in a good mood, and clean, she could crawl on his bed. But only with supervision, as it would be unsafe to leave a baby in the arms of a man who could not lift her, turn her, wipe her nose, catch her before she fell, or otherwise care for her physical needs. So, when she was clean, awake, and happy, and least likely to spit up or leak on him, the family pounced on connecting them. She'd be taken to his chair or bed with the same unpredictability as all infants who rouse their caregivers in the middle of the night, knowing only that they are hungry or wet and therefore demanding immediate attention. My dad only got to hold her when other people burst into his room and said, "She's ready, stop what you are doing!" But grandparents are supposed to get all the moments, too, the ones where the child is just a child. Sometimes stinky, snotty, screaming, and drooling, and sometimes giggling and cuddly. To be with a baby through it all is a gift, and to decide to have a moment together, just the two of you, is a mystical, magical, unspoken joy, and that was never within my dad's control.

Still, he labored valiantly away, tearing down the standard

adult years spent like so many; years spent neglecting the silly, performing, goofy, vulnerable work of playing with a baby. He worked to keep her attention when he couldn't tap on her little feet or blow raspberries in her belly. It must have been exhausting, emotionally, to be restricted to such a small sliver of life with his granddaughter, and never at times of his own choosing.

When Ruth was about eleven months old, before she was really interested in the words that books contain, I bought him a voucher for a create-your-own book. It was something he had done for each of us when we were kids: a book about me riding dinosaurs, a book about the Ninja Turtles for my brother, an illustrated animals-of-the-alphabet for my sister. Some of the things he made for us were hand-drawn, some he sent away to be bound like a proper children's book. So, I offered him one for Ruth. I promised to help craft it, mostly doing the grunt work of illustrating it and navigating the design site for him.

Together, we created a story about little Ruthie, walking through the woods. Ruthie, unable to communicate with any of the fun animals who come by—a fox, a turkey, a fish (whatever I could find from open-source images that looked good with the free backgrounds). Each animal would respond to Ruthie in its own tongue, a fun way to work out sounds, but a sad reality for a lonely girl walking alone in the woods. Until, that is, Ruthie comes across a magic, talking mushroom.

Yes, I am well aware of how that sounds.

The mushroom is John. Grandpa John, that is. And Grandpa John the Mushroom can understand Ruthie. Grandpa John the Mushroom isn't like the animals of the woods. Grandpa John the Mushroom can listen, respond, and talk to Ruthie. But unlike the animals, which come and go as they please, Grandpa John the Mushroom must stay in one spot in the forest, unable to visit Ruthie at her home but never unable to think about her. So while Ruthie must always be the one to physically come visit, the distance between them is eliminated by their intentional decision to think about the other when they aren't in physical proximity.

The book was recorded, with Grandpa John reading all the parts and doing silly voices for the animals, offering a strong, nurturing voice to Ruthie as she learned what it meant that her grandpa was quadriplegic and couldn't come visit Indianapolis, couldn't come watch preschool Christmas choirs, couldn't offer dolphin rides, couldn't hold her, couldn't wipe her tears. Through this recording, Ruth will always have a memory of her grandpa. She will always know that when she was little, he performed for her. And she will grow up with his voice, a voice he rediscovered with months of music and speech therapy, and through becoming a grandparent.

My children will never know that voice. They will hear it on old home movies, and I've ordered extra copies of Ruth's book to keep at my house. But it won't be for them. It won't be speaking to them. It will be a voice that never knew to expect them.

This is a moment of shattered performance. The expectation of fairness for each grandchild, that each would receive roughly equal time with their grandparents, lost. The idea that the younger grandkids would have an impact on their grandfather, impossible. But disability disrupts our timelines, just as it can disrupt the way we live out our lives.

Life is a performance, an idea outlined poignantly by Russian philosopher Mikhail Bakhtin. As we try to live out our ideals, we are always performatively "retelling" the story, rather than "reciting" it. In a traditional classroom, the teacher shares their knowledge with the students; it is a one-way street of information flowing down from the leader to the followers. When they can appropriately recite that information, we deem them as having "learned" enough. But Bakhtin challenges this notion, claiming instead that "truth is not born nor is it to be found inside the head of an individual person, it is born between people collectively searching for truth."[1] Our interactions are what lead us to true learning and true transformation. We have to negotiate and "retell" our lives together, rather than dictate it.

Bakhtin calls life more of a "carnival" than a true performance. A carnival has an element of expected performance, with parades and pageantry, but everyone who is present has a role to play. Even if you are standing on the side, only watching and nothing else, you are still in some sense participating.

When disability has disrupted a life, when a caregiving role is thrust upon you, when the way you interact and perform has changed, it is important to remember that we are never on the sidelines of life. We are always active, performing together, and bearing out truth between one another. To "bear one another's burdens, and thereby fulfill the law of Christ" (Galatians 6:2) is to live together in this way, caring for one another in ways that transform us and point back to God's presence among us. It is not always fun, and often difficult, to view our caregiving relationships as meaningful when we had hoped for a very different performance to play out. But it is unavoidable; we are all always shaking out meaning and learning together.

When you are called into a caregiving role, you are invited to widen the role you play. But you are also invited to see that a major shift in the life of a loved one is no less a role to be performed and an opportunity to shake out truth, together and in new ways.

ACQUIRED

In many ways, we already understand that we are always different from the person we were yesterday. But usually, we call that "growth" or "getting older," or "transformation" if we are really into buzzwords. There is a pervading sense that the changes we experience are connecting pieces between me-at-that-point and me-at-this-point. But when the change is abrupt and happens all at once, we might be tempted to view it as a "disruption" or "break." Me-at-that-point is now on the wrong side of a deep chasm, and me-at-this-point doesn't know how to do anything but slowly lose sight of the way things used to be.

In his 2016 book *Becoming Friends of Time*, a theological inquiry into understanding and welcoming people with severe intellectual disabilities, advanced dementia, and acquired brain injuries, John Swinton notes how people struggle against the feeling that a brain injury separates the old person from before from the new person after—a sufficiently traumatic injury can break the perception that we are singular entities crossing time.[2] Writing alongside his friend Tonya, who has an acquired brain injury, Swinton writes about how after an accident you are in the world in a different way than you were before.

Much like in death, the old you is no longer accessible to the people who loved you, or even to yourself. Only the memory really remains. But unlike in death, the person is still physically here. Their body is still moving through this world. Much like a ghost, their abrupt change can remind us of the certainty of death and the uncertainty it brings, causing fear and trepidation. Tonya describes this as a "live death," a sense of estrangement from both yourself and with others.

When my dad died, there was a pregnant question on the lips of those too polite to ask: "Aren't you relieved that he's finally gone?" No one asked this, not directly. But I could feel the question in the ways they would start to move their tongue inside their mouths before thinking better of it. I could hear it when they were just a little too quick to agree when we'd name some small silver lining. It sounds harsh to claim that people who knew and loved my father would hold such an expectation, that we'd breathe a sigh of relief when he was no longer in our lives. But I think I understand why that question sits heavy on the heart, even if it can't be asked out loud.

When my dad fell, his neck broke. And when it did, part of who he was instantly left. The John Endress who loved hiking, who wanted to spend his retirement roaming through Great Smoky Mountains National Park, who played in a tennis league and went for long bike rides, the John who was famous at the gym for pushing himself so hard on the elliptical machine that even years later the front desk worker brought up to me how awful it was to clean the sweat after he used it—that John was gone. Inaccessible. Estranged. Dead. More than nine years before he died in his hospice room, a big portion of him died on that mountain.

An acquired brain injury might disrupt your body, as in the

case of a C3 spinal fracture. But it might cause different issues. A stroke might cause the left side of your body to stop responding to your brain. A virus could disrupt synaptic connections and cause memory loss. Anything that your brain controls, from vision to language to movement to taste, it's all subject to disruption by a brain injury. But when one or more of these are significantly changed, it can feel like the entire person has been lost, even when they are still right in front of us. It's disorienting and uncomfortable. It blurs the lines between life and death in ways we can't control. A man in a power wheelchair, who used to love to move and run and swing a racquet and cycle and play basketball, challenges us to see how the things we love will one day be inaccessible to us, too.

When people were relieved that my dad died, it doesn't mean they were happy to see him go. But I do think that at some level they were happy to not have to be confronted with the reality that their lives, my life, our lives, are short and end without our consent. Life is supposed to happen uninterrupted until death, and then you are dealing with something else. You might not know what it is, but it isn't the life we know now, and everyone knows it. It's a clean break. But spinal cord injuries and acquired disabilities aren't like that. Rather, they open a space between life and death, dragging out what should be a momentary state of dying and turning it into a sustained pattern of life.

For Tonya, this fearsome and uncomfortable liminality was closed thanks to a funeral held for "old Tonya," which allowed friends to say good-bye to the parts of her that were radically changed by her brain injury while welcoming in her new self. Had we done something like that for my dad, maybe it would have been easier to more fully mourn when he fully died. But what if the person doesn't want to mark that change? What if they are happy to do all the physical therapy in the world, use every resource and support they can find, but never want to identify with their disability? For my dad, frankly, the idea of holding a funeral for his preaccident body would have been more akin to being buried alive.

The way in which we accompany one another is a performance, a dance or duet, where we must listen to what the other is saying or doing. For Tonya, her accompanists could hear her need for marking a disjunction in her life, and they responded in kind. They acknowledged the need for a pause, a break, taking a new breath before starting off on a new musical phrase.

For my father, this would have been out of tune. As we build toward the skill of listening to one another, truly responding to the needs and desires of those around us becomes a means of grace and a means of building God's kingdom on earth. Setting down our own desires for how someone else lives their life in favor of taking a backseat, augmenting their melody and highlighting their own agency even in our mutual dependence, is how God calls us to care for one another.

To listen to someone well enough to know what they need is a skill that requires development. By virtue of being a caregiver, you are flexing that muscle already. Doing so with more intention will help transform that skill in practical ways.

First, we have to lay down our own desires that cloud our understanding of what another person really needs. Often, we hear what we want to hear, and other times we hear what we expect. If we can acknowledge that the person we are accompanying is, at least in part, different from who they were before we began this caregiving relationship, it can be easier to set aside the expectations we have for them. When children age and become more independent, it can be a challenge for parents to see them as full adults with independent desires and skills; likewise, seeing the development of our loved ones is only really possible when we lay down our tight grasps on seeing the person they once were.

Second, we have to choose to be humble. The humility required to be a true caregiver prevents us from developing a "savior complex," in which we begin to view ourselves as some wonderful gift to a needy person. You are a gift, but so is everyone else. Our relationships have to be equitable, and for that we need to set down any desire to dominate or own all the responsibility for someone else. Practice asking someone you give care to for help; this is one of the best ways to force yourself to see your own limitations—and their gifts.

Finally, accept that perfection is a myth, but practice is worthwhile anyway. You will never perfectly meet someone's needs, but actual accompaniment requires us to first and foremost be our authentic selves, not perfect care robots. Spend time working on things like offering encouraging words, asking for clarity rather than assuming what people need, listening more, and praying for understanding.

The more we listen to one another, without pretense and expectation, the better we can respond to each other.

Downtown

AFP was located in the Chicago suburbs and the Rehabilitation Institute of Chicago (RIC) lies in the heart of the city. The two institutions are just twenty miles apart, but they were worlds apart in terms of the quality of care they provided me. From day one at RIC, I saw patients eagerly working out in the hallways, people decorating a Christmas tree, and doctors and specialists engaged in their work. It instantly felt like a safe place where I could focus on healing.

Sometime after my arrival at RIC, I met Ryan. Ryan was from Eldorado, Illinois, a town not too far from Evansville. As unbelievable as it may sound, many businesses in the small, rural town of Eldorado were rumored by my coworkers, based on conjecture and myth, to be owned by the Mafia. But Ryan was as far from the Mafia as a guy could get.

Ryan was a patient at RIC because he suffered from transverse myelitis, an autoimmune disease that perceives the sheath that insulates the spinal cord as a foreign body and begins to attack its cells. He was sitting in his grandmother's living room watching television, then, with no warning, was on the floor and gasping to breathe. After medical diagnosis and treatment in Evansville, Ryan served time in AFP hell before being transferred to RIC, just like me.

Our therapy was at the same time and we got to know each other well. Cherry and Ryan's mom became great friends. Ryan was my partner in crime. Before we left RIC, one of our assignments was to go out to eat and return successfully. We drove ourselves (in our wheelchairs, of course) to a mall just up the street. While each of us was escorted by a therapist, it was still a bit nerve-racking to be away from the security of RIC.

After we each returned home, he was hospitalized in Evansville and I went to visit him. He was on a ventilator and not able to operate his wheelchair. My visit boosted Ryan and his dad's spirits as my progress gave them hope that a functional recovery was possible. Topher later worked as a chaplain at the hospital where Ryan often lived, and they would visit together at length, which I always thought was nice for them.

Although RIC was filled with excellent nurses, doctors, occupational therapists, and physical therapists, it was not a hospital. At one point, I asked that my neck brace be removed, which required an MRI scan to see if my neck was strong enough. I was wheeled through a tunnel across the street to Northwestern Hospital; it was a terrible experience, and not just because Northwestern is a Big Ten rival to my alma mater, Purdue. When I returned to RIC, my doctor informed me that there was something suspicious in the pictures Northwestern had taken. We were sent back to Northwestern, by ambulance this time despite being just a couple of hundred feet away, and ushered into the emergency room. There was no gurney big enough for me, so Cherry had to hold me so I wouldn't fall off.

Given that I was laying down, unable to speak or see much at all, my perception of the hospital is shaped by confusion, fear, uncertainty, and a feeling of chaos. It seemed like there were numerous gunshot victims pouring into the ER, which made sense given the downtown location and its status as the premier trauma center for the metro area. It felt like a war zone, and we received little attention. At some point, after they had admitted me but before they found there to be no stroke, I developed a fever and was diagnosed with pneumonia. Although the fever did not last, it recurred daily. I couldn't be released until they had cleared me, which meant growing cultures, running extra tests, and waiting. The hospital was, for reasons I do not fully remember, unable to put in my speaking valve, leaving me unable to talk during these frantic several days. Each day that passed was one more day of regression, and Cherry was often forced to fight against well-meaning, caring staff who in their individual brilliance seemed to miss *my* bigger picture.

I needed rehab, and beds at RIC are rare. By this point, Cherry had accompanied me through enough tests, scans, hospital rounds, and consultations that she had become an expert herself and spent several days arguing that my periodic fevers were likely a result of my damaged nervous system and not an infection. She was later proven correct, but in the meantime, Northwestern wanted to continue to run tests on me. Despite their insistence on keeping me, they still moved slower than we wanted. It took them three days to insert a peripherally inserted central catheter (PICC) line. That PICC line, however, caused a clot and resulted in three or four ultrasounds being conducted each day. For this, I am convinced I served as a useful teaching tool for the numerous medical students there. After five days of this confusion, Cherry called my doctor at RIC to see if he could convince them to release me. It was only then that Cherry discovered that reports from the hospital had somehow given RIC the impression that I was unresponsive or incapable of rehab, despite very clear evidence to the contrary, and they'd given away my bed. Eventually, Cherry was able to connect the medical teams and fought for me to be readmitted to RIC for further rehab.

Although the individuals who worked with me were caring and excellent at their tasks, the unique challenge of my injury made it impossible for me to advocate for my own needs. Everyone needs an advocate, no matter how good their hospital or doctor may be. This situation could have been a death sentence for me without the intervention and advocacy of my family.

Once back at RIC, music became part of my speech therapy. During one session, I shared with my speech therapist that I used to play the harmonica. She told me that this would be good therapy. Subsequently I asked Cherry to get me a harmonica and a neck holder. From that point forward, the harmonica was instrumental in my therapy. One day, when my doctor was making his rounds, he heard me playing. In no time at all he had filled my room and the hallway with doctors, nurses, and technicians for an impromptu recital. The song I played was "Faded Love," a Bob Wills classic.

RIC also had a full-time music therapist on staff. She was a very petite Asian-American woman who spoke perfect English but with a very thick accent. She played the guitar while all of the patients sang along. Her song choices seemed, to me, quite eclectic. Her first selection was Johnny Cash's "Folsom Prison Blues." The second choice was "Clementine." The two songs couldn't be further apart. It was quite humorous to listen to ex-trach patients, none with strong voices, sing these songs as the therapist sang right along, thick accent and all. It only took one session for me to decide this wasn't for me. Nevertheless, I left with a fond memory.

As I was regaining a voice, I also began to hope for a day when I could eat on my own. At AFP, I attempted and failed two swallowing tests. As a result, I had some trepidation when it came time to take a swallowing test at RIC. As it turned out, the two experiences could not have been more different. First, instead of a mean nurse strapping me to an uncomfortable board at an odd angle, I simply sat in a normal position. And instead of having an insensitive technician look at the monitor and tell me that I failed, the monitor was placed where the technicians and I could both see it. When I completed the test, I asked whether I had passed or failed. I was told that there is no way to fail a swallowing test since the purpose is to see how much progress I had made and what techniques I still had to work on. Because everyone involved was so positive, I left the test with the optimistic expectation that I would eventually be able to eat on my own.

7

Accompaniment

Theology, Shaken Out One Step at a Time

It is still jarring to me how regularly people of deep faith and conviction, who have been worshiping in churches for decades, will tell me they "don't know anything about theology." As if their many years of loving commitment to God's kingdom is somehow totally separate from the work of describing God.

So often we ascribe so much importance to a very academic conception of God that we concede all of our God-talk to the folks with the fanciest words and most diplomas, as if the smartest people are always the holiest. I hope you realize how absolutely untrue this is. God is best communicated *about* when communicated *with* through prayer and worship. I use the word "communicate" rather than "talk" because so often, our communication extends far beyond the words we might utter.

The Revs. Mindi Welton-Mitchell and J. C. Mitchell, married but pastoring in different denominations, write about their son A.J. and his relationship with church while communicating nonverbally. "A.J. claps, shakes hands, laughs, and gets excited when others do during the worship service. In a way, he is professing his faith through the body language that he observed from participating with others. . . . we are not one hundred percent certain of A.J.'s motives . . . but we are reminded that in Augmentative and Alternative Communication, we are to consider all of his forms of communication as an attempt to express himself. He may very well be in tune with the Spirit in the worship service."[1] Being attuned to the Spirit is to be practicing theology, verbal or not.

Theologian Roberto Goizueta reminds the world that in Latino/a culture, and ideally everywhere, "religious faith is virtually indistinguishable from our everyday relationship with Jesus and Mary, lived out in everything from the most highly 'institutional' liturgical services to the most intimate, personal devotions—and every aspect of life in between."[2] There is no division between the God described by the ten-dollar words of academia, hidden within dense books and peer-reviewed journals, the God praised within the biggest cathedrals, and the God worshiped in the deeply personal faith lives of devoted Christians living ordinary lives.

All of us, Latinx or not, are not just allowed to talk about God, but offered the opportunity to *embody* our theology in such a way that our lives are spent engaging in this God-talk.

To be accompanied by the incarnate word, the person of Christ, who is both the Jesus of history and the triune God, is to allow yourself the freedom to name that God is at work in you, and therefore you are the site of theology. Not textbooks, or ancient scrolls buried in the desert, or seminary lecture halls—*you*. The resurrection not only came about in history but is centered on the still-living Christ. Breaking bread together reminds us that Christ *was* and that Christ *is* and that Christ *will be*, and that Christ is through all of this *with* us. We are accompanied by the risen Christ in our current spaces, wherever we go. As Goizueta notes, "it is not our Christian belief that makes God's nearness credible. Rather, it is God's nearness that makes Christian belief . . . credible."[3] The holiness that flows from God's nearness in our lives exposes our vulnerabilities and confronts us with the real experiences of death; it is not for nothing that the Hebrew response to a vision of God was to assume that God's perfection was going to utterly annihilate their imperfection (and their lives, with it). Who can stand in the presence of the Almighty? Certainly not me!

However, the Christian liturgical response to the risk of death is to gather together in community to eat and drink again, saying, "This holy thing is for you." All holy things are given a place. The Bible offers up cities of refuge, which emerge to give place even to murderers, because even murderers are human and all humans are holy things.[4] Yet where today are the cities of refuge for those with disabilities? Where are the places where they can simply exist without struggle, spaces where eating and gathering in community are still possible? Are the streets, unfriendly to bodies and filled with an ever-increasing onslaught of cars, a potential site for holy bodies to dwell together? Are buildings of culture, like libraries and museums and schools, hidden behind staircases, heavy doors, and a vast network of unwritten rules a potential sacred place for the neurodiverse? Can the institutions, hospitals, and nursing homes into which many disabled people are forced become a place where the holy circle is truly wide enough?

Does Jesus really dwell in the churches if no disabilities are welcomed and invited to share the meal?

Anyone who is accompanied by God is a theologian, because they are living lives that are constantly speaking of God. Why should we ever presume that the disabled faithful are any less the site of God's presence than anyone else? When we put it this way, the answer is obvious: we shouldn't. Disabled Christians are not distinct from able-bodied Christians when it comes to anyone's capacity for holiness, faithfulness, love, and grace. The reasons we have for drawing lines between a disabled Christian and God don't stem from theological requirements, but from our overly restrictive social imaginations. When our spaces and programs are designed without including disabled worship as foundational to the work of the people of God, the church begins to look like the unfriendly, ableist world. Our supposed sanctuaries become dead spaces indistinct from any supermarket or department store.

Your life itself can be theology because God is at work in the story—not just historically, but in the telling and sharing itself. Thus, John's story is theology, one of untold billions. How much deeper would our understanding of God be if only we could truly attend to the people who accompany us, all of those who find Christ walking with them on their journey? Can we truly have ears to hear, eyes to see, and minds to comprehend the way that God is at work in the lives of those we care for?

God is found not only in soaring towers but also in prison cells, nursing homes, isolated back alleys, and lonely apartments where people sit excluded from society. Even the hardest and most oppressive of spaces can be redeemed into a site of holy worship; the furnace of Nebuchadnezzar was transformed into a site of worship by the presence of the angel, the action of the Jewish youths, and, as the Rev. Dr. Martin Luther King Jr. notes, the holy act of civil disobedience.[5] Places like sheltered institutions, dingy nursing home rooms, and segregated classrooms, even though they have been used to harm and oppress, can be made new into a site of God's presence when those present are met by the accompanying Spirit of God. Disabled lives, with the restrictions on movement and travel that often follow, demand a broad definition of "space" to include online worship, video calls with family, communities that emerge over texting and social media, all accessed from a bed. How can we sing our songs on foreign shores, in spaces unfamiliar, hidden, and undesired?

But we can sing, and we must.

Catholic theologian Aidan Kavanagh offers insight into how the senses might fit together to make meaning beyond merely the sum of the parts.

> The history of Christian faith is also the history of the ear, the eye, the body in gesture and movement, the taste, and the kinesthetic reception of God. Wherever the community gathers to hear the word and to bring life to worship, the consequences are poetic, metaphoric, and visionary. What is presented to the senses carries beyond the literally given. . . . Despite all temptations to the contrary, Christian liturgy remains a practice of the human body at full stretch. This

means that crossing over our senses of seeing, hearing, tasting, touching, and moving can reveal more than meets the eye or ear or tongue alone.[6]

No one body holds authority in worship. There is no "perfect churchgoer" mold that we all ought to fit into. No one has a body that can hold all the width of *the body*, aside from Christ. We need each other to participate if we are to worship in fullness.

Such an acknowledgment also helps us deemphasize specific actions in favor of a plurality of expressions that account for ritual meaning; in other words, Communion might not be accessible to everyone, nor is congregational singing, nor is listening to a thirty-minute academic sermon. It is entirely reasonable to expect, and even demand, accommodations to make worship accessible. But what if access itself is not safe? If you are caring for someone with an eating disorder, organizing one's faith participation around a food ritual might be restorative for them, but it might also be unsafe and triggering. If we can reframe worship around a focus on multisensory engagement, we can allow people to participate where and how they can in ways that are safe and supportive to them. Those who find traditional praxis inaccessible (like a quadriplegic being asked to "please rise and sing the next hymn," or those with celiac disease attempting to take Roman Catholic Communion, which by canon law cannot be made without gluten, or the socially anxious person being asked to pass the peace) may find alternative expressions through other senses and actions. This must be tackled communally, because what one participant does in worship impacts the whole body. We all hold responsibility to navigate the balance between accommodating different practical needs and uplifting alternate rituals with no loss in meaning so that the entire community can worship in the fullness of their lived experience.

God is not met in our worship by achieving some exact standard of musical perfection, nor by offering a contextually perfect sermon, nor by everyone reading the texts without stumbling over words. Worship is dependent on both the movement of the same Spirit who moves across history and the bodily reality of those humans who engage in worship. And we all can participate at the pace that works for us, together.

A service that cannot offer someone with a body like John the space to worship is not a service offered to God. But a service that acknowledges that we all always bring our diverse bodies to worship provides us the surety that God meets each of us exactly where we are. In the truly inclusive church, the bodies of those who do not move on their own—bodies like my father's—ought never be expected to bear alone the weight of an actively moving Spirit.

In the understanding of the communal body of Christ acting as the church, however, the bodies of those with quadriplegia and those who lack external sensory connections are uniquely positioned to inform the other. The solidarity that forms from acknowledging the political aspect of disabled life can strengthen the interconnectedness of the body at worship. And the ways that accompanists are formed and re-formed by the journeys of those they love pulse with the same energy that God offers to us. The movement of one who can move can act as the conduit of the Spirit, and the one who can see can be their interpreter of the world around them. When we gather in all our diversity, attentive to the ways God has moved in each other's lives, we accept the potentiality for the Spirit to, in real time and among real life, accompany us in such a way as to transform our individualities, communities, and entire world as we produce space alongside those on the margins.

Following God, the accompanists, the caregivers, the parents and siblings—the people who care deeply for a disabled person—seek a solidarity that mirrors God's willingness to die a grotesque death on the cross. God did not come to earth as a symbol of every person, but *as* a person, with a particular set of features and connection to the political, economic, and social world that forms the boundaries of our definition of "disability" to begin with. Christ was marginal, a poor man born to a poor family with no political clout and little social status. God's own praxis is enacted in the margins, giving us a theology of accompaniment in which the church's worship "really is in contact with the homes and the lives of its people, and does not become a useless structure out of touch with people or a self-absorbed group made up of a chosen few."[7]

Where two or more are gathered together, assembled for the purpose of God's work, Christ is present (Matthew 18:20). No further constraints ought to be made on the manner in which this assembly forms. Looking into New Testament narratives, one finds instances of authentic communities forming irrespective of social location, identity markers, or abilities.

Early on in the fledgling church's life, just after the ascension of Christ to heaven, as the disciples and followers are figuring out how to attend to one another and live into this new faith, Philip is sent by the Spirit into Gaza (Acts 8:26–40). There, he encounters an Ethiopian eunuch, a court official who had been trusted enough to make the long trek from Africa to Jerusalem. He was privileged as an official, but also marginal as a eunuch, a man who had his testicles removed so as to serve a queen without fear of complicating any relationships or bloodlines. He was to be the first recorded Gentile convert to the newly formed Christian movement. With the Spirit of the Lord abundantly present, Philip baptizes him on the road, widening the presence of God's kingdom in line with the more universal promises of Scripture (see Psalm 68:31; Matthew 22:9). Rather than limiting the experience of two coming together in the work of God, the physical location (a chariot on a dirt road, far from Jerusalem) and demographics of the two men (a poor, able-bodied Jewish man and a rich Ethiopian eunuch) never cause disruption in the ability of the Spirit to remain present.

Under early Jewish law, a man with wounded and significantly damaged testicles was forbidden from entering into the assembly of God (Deuteronomy 23:1). This was "overturned" in God's message in Isaiah 56, in which God explicitly names foreigners and eunuchs as partaking in the kingdom. This is made good in the ministry of Philip, as the presence of the Spirit is clear in her command to teach and include despite the disabling social and cultural understanding of Gentiles and genitals that would otherwise prohibit this interaction. Philip is placed in physical proximity to and engages with the unnamed eunuch in the work of God, with the Spirit abundantly present; how dare we claim that this is not the very embodiment of the church! The work of the church—teaching, thanksgiving, and sending out in order to perform its duty as the herald of Christ's conquering of death—is performed without limitation regardless of physical embodiment.

Rather than allowing the social and architectural constructs to dictate action and thought, it is incumbent on us as Christians to recognize that no building, label, or practice holds authority to limit the assembling of God's people. An autistic man, a woman with Down syndrome, a person with cerebral palsy, a Deaf child, a sister born blind, a schizophrenic man, and a father with quadriplegia all have unique needs as they exist within the world. To accompany any of them is to extend to them the light of God, and to allow them to extend that light to others, recognizing that authentic community necessarily values the ways in which a body takes space. Thus, Revelation 7:9–10 becomes a commandment to ensure that relationships can exist in every context for every body, tongue, and ability:

> After these things I looked (or listened), and behold, a great multitude which no one could count, from every nation and all the tribes, peoples, and languages, standing (and sitting in their wheelchairs) before the throne and before the Lamb, clothed in white robes, and palm branches were in their hands (and being held by their attendants); and they cried out with a loud voice, saying (or signing), "Salvation belongs to our God who sits on the throne, and to the Lamb!" (NASB, alt. T. Endress)

May this be, on earth as it is in heaven.

A Life Well Lived

Two years after my accident, things are going well, just extremely busy. I continue to do therapy at Easter Seals, my local rehabilitation center, four days a week. I have had the same four therapists for this whole time. They are very dedicated and very skilled. At some points, they feel like friends who are accompanying me through my workouts rather than my therapists. In addition, my brother Steve comes by three times a week and we do therapy at home. This takes a lot of time out of his schedule, and I appreciate it.

For a long time, I've had what is called an e-stim (electronic stimulation) bicycle. It's a stationary bike that I pull up to in my chair. It works arms and legs, although so far I've only been working with arms. It's a pretty sophisticated machine that sends current through appropriate muscles to stimulate them while I'm riding. I've only recently gotten approval from the doctors to ride it. It feels good to be exercising again. It took Cherry and my doctors months of arguing with the insurance company about getting it covered, so I am happy to use it, knowing how hard they worked to make it available to me.

I spend quite a bit of time on my computer. It's been a very frustrating process getting it to work with voice recognition, but I think I've got it working pretty well now. The program I use is apparently designed for doctors and lawyers to dictate notes, but lying in bed at strange angles makes it difficult to sound as professional as the computer seems to want. Often, it records long strings of gibberish or else it simply doesn't pick up on my voice at all. I am able to do many things independently, but it is far easier to have someone type for me.

I have volunteers who take me to therapy at Easter Seals and come by to visit regularly. My sister-in-law Mag, Cherry's parents Pete and Virginia, my sister-in-law Cindy, my brother Thom, my friends Jimmy and Jodie, lots of people from church, and my friend Jeff all help out a lot during the day while Cherry is working. And of course, my two Evansville-dwelling children, Emily and Michael, help out frequently. Topher now lives in Nashville but is a big help when he comes home.

Topher typically sleeps on the couch in my room whenever he visits, turning me every two hours overnight to prevent bed-sores. In the morning, someone has to get me cereal and feed me, which is a slow process. I like to chew thoroughly to limit the chance of choking. I also do stretches every morning, with someone pulling my arms and legs to help keep my posture. My muscles are frequently incredibly tight, and often I have painful spasms akin to whole-body muscle cramps. I am looking into having a pump inserted into my back that can offer a regular release of Baclofen, a drug that can help with this. Until then, stretching is a necessary, and again time-consuming, practice.

Getting into my chair sometimes takes multiple attempts. I have to be angled correctly, with the chair tilted back, before being lowered down and shifted. My head needs to reach my head array, which allows me to control my chair. If I am slouched or tilted too far to either side, I cannot control my chair to either move or adjust how high off the ground I am. I often misjudge my footpads and scrape the floor or sidewalk, but am, in Topher's words, "surprisingly good at not knocking things over" when I drive.

I've been doing a little work with my old company but am somewhat limited because of all the time I spend at therapy and my inability to go to the field. I've also maintained my membership on several boards and find that rewarding.

Thanks again for everyone's support and interest. I hope all of you are doing well.

A Final Note

John passed in 2019, nearly seven years after this last note was written. I included it at the end to leave you with a hopeful, yet accurate, note: no matter the circumstance, the Spirit of God never leaves us to fend for ourselves. Life continues on. The challenges faced by my father over the final decade of his life are uncommon, yet the struggle we all face is exposed in the universal realities of his journey.

Disability theology is the work of sharing about God in light of a personal, political, communal, economic, and social experience known as "disability." This involves pain, exclusion, joy, creativity, and everything in between. Although it is not a single shape, it is also not shapeless. There are boundaries around it; not everyone is disabled. Still, we are all limited and must contend with bodies that do not do the things that we want them to.

It is my sincere hope that this book would help in a few ways. First, I wrote this to offer hope to those who are giving care right now. To the woman caring for her husband who has late-stage Alzheimer's disease. The young couple rearing a child with oppositional defiant disorder. The child navigating a parent's cognitive decline. The sibling vying for her family's attention despite the complex medical needs of her brother. I see you. I know you. I am you. Your stories matter, and God is in the midst of it with you. Just as you accompany your loved ones and are marked by their presence in your life, God accompanies you.

Second, I hope this book equips you to talk more directly about the experience of disability in your own life. If there really is something about accompaniment that can be explained by focusing on time, narrative, history, space, and performance, but cannot be fully covered by these lenses, maybe reading John's story and my reflections will equip you to better discern what God is doing in your life, and in the lives of the people around you.

How have you accompanied someone in their journey? Who has accompanied you? Where do you find God at work in your life, and how can you be attentive to what God is doing? These are great questions for reflection for all of us.

Finally, I hope this provides us some improved language that allows us to begin drawing a more distinct division between work that is "disability theology" and work that is "accompaniment theology," without making one the "better" field. We need to learn from disabled people, and likewise we need to learn from those who provide care and companionship along the way.

God is with us. Let us be with one another, as well.

Acknowledgments

One of the themes running through this book is that no one goes it alone. That is doubly true about writing a book, as it is for life in general. No list of names could sufficiently highlight all of the people who made this book possible, but generally speaking, if you knew my father and at least made some attempt to bring light, joy, and friendship to his postaccident life, you played a major role in shaping this book. Thank you for all the ways you accompanied John, both small and large, intermittent or ongoing.

The team at Westminster John Knox was fantastic to work with. My editor Jessica Miller Kelley deserves a heap of praise for reining in my overwriting, and for her keen insights both structural and theological as I drafted this book.

To my friends and colleagues at the University of Aberdeen, who helped me craft a theological voice—sometimes in a seminar, sometimes in worship, and sometimes at a pub after a long run—thank you for the deep care you extended to me for such a long period of this book's gestation. In particular, my PhD cohort, the Hillview community, Aberdeen Inspire, Metro Aberdeen Running Club, and of course everyone in the Aberdeen Friendship House.

To my Vanderbilt family, for the ways you taught me to view the world with a big heart, an unrelenting spirit, and a critical eye, and to Purdue, for giving me a loving community to accompany me through my dad's initial accident.

To my current community in Columbia, Missouri, including my family (even when you don't let me sleep) and my church family at First Christian. Thank you for equipping me to continuously grow as a person, a minister, a leader, and a follower.

Finally, to my mother, who modeled how to be a caregiver through the long years, and even longer days, of accompanying my father through the daily grind. Thank you for all of the teaching, both direct and indirect, you've provided me over the years.

Book Club Discussion Guide

1. Have you ever considered yourself a theologian? What do you find meaningful about the distinction between disability theology and accompaniment theology?

2. Do you have a preference between the terms "person with a disability" and "disabled person"? Did the author's discussion of both terms' value on page 14 cause you to reconsider that preference?

3. What role does disability play in how you describe yourself or tell your life story? Do you imagine a certain version of yourself or your loved one as ideal or essential that is lost in disability or regained in the afterlife?

4. What could people learn from the author's comparison of how we view parents caring for new babies and caregivers accompanying disabled loved ones? What about the way we see God in the relationships between caregiver and care receiver?

5. Chapters 3 and 4 discuss ethical questions around assisted suicide, medical decision making, prenatal testing, and abortion. Did the book change the way you think about any of those issues?

6. Had you ever considered the way the Bible's stories of Jesus healing people may be read by people with disabilities, or the impact of praying for a person's healing? How should we approach the idea of divine healing?

7. What was the most memorable or impactful story, anecdote, or example in the book? Why did it stand out to you?

8. Did the book change the way you see (or will try to see) the mundane, difficult, and even gross parts of caregiving? How might this impact your relationships with God and with other people?

9. Did the inclusion of John's own writing give you any new insight on disability or the work of accompaniment?

10. What are some of the questions or criticisms you have about the book? What would you ask or tell the author if you had the opportunity?

Notes

Introduction

1. "Deaf" is often capitalized because it describes a cultural identity more than just a difference in function. Many Deaf people consider themselves different from hearing people, both as individuals and as a culture, but they would not consider themselves disabled. Alternatively, someone who loses their hearing later in life may not identify with the language(s), school systems, and collective history of the Deaf community. A deaf person may consider their audiological function difference to be a medical condition and/or disability.

2. The term "quadriplegic" refers to a person affected by a spinal cord injury that impacts sensation, function, and/or movement across all the limbs of the body. Increasingly, the term "tetraplegic" is replacing "quadriplegic," but I stick with the latter given that it is how our family and my dad's team of health-care professionals referred to his condition.

Chapter 1: Narrative

1. This statistic from the Centers for Disease Control and Prevention (CDC) is based on respondents' self-reporting in answers to questions of function. The study asked questions like "Do you have serious difficulty walking or climbing stairs?" rather than "Do you have an ambulatory disability?" It is possible that relying on functional assessments gives a higher percentage of responses than a survey that asks if people identify with the term "disabled." This matters a great deal for how ministers, chaplains, and caregivers address people and their needs. See https://www.cdc.gov/ncbddd/disabilityandhealth/features/disability-health-data.html.

2. Roberto S. Goizueta, *Caminemos con Jesús: Toward a Hispanic/Latino Theology of Accompaniment* (Maryknoll, NY: Orbis Books, 1995) 49.

3. See Brian Brock, "Theologizing Inclusion: 1 Corinthians 12 and the Politics of the Body of Christ," *Journal of Religion, Disability & Health* 15, no. 4 (2011): 351–76, https://doi.org/10.1080/15228967.2011.620389; Brian Brock and Bernd Wannenwetsch, *The Malady of the Christian Body: A Theological Exposition of Paul's First Letter to the Corinthians, Volume 1* (Eugene, OR: Cascade Books, 2016); and Brock and Wannenwetsch, *The Therapy of the Christian Body: A Theological Exposition of Paul's First Letter to the Corinthians, Volume 2* (Eugene, OR: Cascade Books, 2018).

4. Naoki Higashida, *The Reason I Jump: The Inner Voice of a Thirteen-Year-Old Boy with Autism,* trans. KA Yoshida and David Mitchell (New York: Random House, 2013 [Japanese original, 2007]).

5. Jordyn Zimmerman, *This Is Not about Me*, directed by Marco Niemeijer (2021).

Chapter 2: Time

1. Ellen Samuels, "Six Ways of Looking at Crip Time," *Disability Studies Quarterly* 37, no. 3 (August 31, 2017), https://doi.org/10.18061/dsq.v37i3.5824.

2. Andrew Irving, "Life Made Strange: An Essay on the Re-inhabitation of Bodies and Landscapes," in *The Qualities of Time: Anthropological Approaches,* ed. Wendy James and David Mills (Oxford: Berg, 2005), 317–29.

3. Samuels, "Six Ways."

Chapter 3: Economy

1. Deborah Beth Creamer, *Disability and Christian Theology: Embodied Limits and Constructive Possibilities* (New York: Oxford University Press, 2009).

2. Roberto S. Goizueta, *Christ Our Companion: Toward a Theological Aesthetics of Liberation* (Maryknoll, NY: Orbis Books, 2009), 68.

3. IDD is the standard abbreviation for intellectual and developmental disabilities, a wide term describing congenital conditions that impact cognition.

4. Stella Young, "I'm Not Your Inspiration, Thank You Very Much," TED Talk, Sydney, Australia, posted June 9, 2014, https://www.ted.com/talks/stella_young_i_m_not_your_inspiration_thank_you_very_much.

5. Travis Pickell, "What's Going On in Canada with Assisted Suicide?," *Church Life Journal*, January 12, 2024.

6. Amir Farsoud, "I Couldn't Afford to Live, So I Asked Doctors to Help Me Die—and They Said Yes," *Independent*, November 27, 2022, https://www.independent.co.uk/voices/assisted-dying-maid-suicide-canada-homeless-b2233845.html.

7. D. E. Saliers, "Liturgy and Ethics: Some New Beginnings," *Journal of Religious Ethics* 7, no. 2 (Fall 1979): 174.

8. Charles Weijer, "A Death in the Family: Reflections on the Terri Schiavo Case," *Canadian Medical Association Journal* 172, no. 9 (April 2005): 1197–98.

9. Rebecca Coombes, "Ashley X: A Difficult Moral Choice," *BMJ* 334, no. 7584 (January 2007): 72–73.

10. Nancy Eiesland, "Liberation, Inclusion, and Justice: A Faith Response to Persons with Disabilities," *Impact* 14, no. 3 (Winter 2001/2002).

11. Creamer, *Disability and Christian Theology.*

Chapter 4: History

1. Evrim Altintas and Oriel Sullivan, "Fifty Years of Change Updated: Cross-National Gender Convergence in Housework," *Demographic Research* 35 (2016): 455–70, http://www.jstor.org/stable/26332084.

2. "Can't Grow Old without Her: Women's Central Role in a Growing Eldercare Economy," Economics, Wells Fargo, March 5, 2024, https://wellsfargo.bluematrix.com/links2/html/0b9c0833-906b-41e0-82f9-7406ae95cf72.

3. William Wordsworth, "My Heart Leaps Up," available at https://poets.org/poem/my-heart-leaps.

4. Mélodie Kauffmann, "Job's Wife Urged Him to 'Curse God and Die.' Caregivers Get It," *Christianity Today*, January 26, 2023, https://www.christianitytoday.com/2023/01/job-wife-curse-god-die-caregiver-suffering/.

5. Bethany McKinney Fox, *Disability and the Way of Jesus: Holistic Healing in the Gospels and the Church* (Downers Grove, IL: IVP Academic, 2019), 46.

6. "Spinal Cord Injury," World Health Organization, April 16, 2024, https://www.who.int/news-room/fact-sheets/detail/spinal-cord-injury.

7. National Spinal Cord Injury Statistical Center, "SCIMS 2023 Annual Report—Complete Public Version," https://www.nscisc.uab .edu/Public/AR2023_public%20version.pdf.

Chapter 5: Space

1. Yes, in Paris, it is expresso, not espresso. Is there a difference between an Italian espresso and a French expresso? I cannot tell, but then, I also drink instant coffee most days, so my palate is apparently not to be trusted.

2. Elizabeth Guffey, *Designing Disability: Symbols, Space, and Society* (London: Bloomsbury Visual Arts, 2018).

3. Thomas F. Torrance, *Space, Time and Incarnation* (New York: Oxford University Press, 1969), 75.

4. I (Topher) must add that this carelessness led to ventilators being unplugged, the gastronomy tube coming loose, skin breaks and bedsores developing, and John being left alone with no way to call for help (ventilator) or page a nurse (can't move arms to reach a call button) for eight-plus hours at a time. "Dangerous" undersells it quite a bit.

Chapter 6: Performance

1. Mikhail Bakhtin, *Problems of Dostoevsky's Poetics*, trans. Caryl Emerson (Minneapolis: University of Minnesota Press, 1984), 110.

2. John Swinton, *Becoming Friends of Time: Disability, Timefullness, and Gentle Discipleship* (London: SCM Press, 2017).

Chapter 7: Accompaniment

1. Mindi Welton-Mitchell and J. C. Mitchell, "Nonverbal Proclamations of Faith," *Christian Citizen*, May 29, 2023, https://christiancitizen.us/nonverbal-proclamations-of-faith/.

2. Roberto S. Goizueta, *Caminemos con Jesús: Toward a Hispanic/ Latino Theology of Accompaniment* (Maryknoll, NY: Orbis Books, 1995), 30.

3. Roberto S. Goizueta, "The Symbolic Realism of U.S. Latino/a Popular Catholicism," *Theological Studies* 65 (2004): 267.

4. Gordon W. Lathrop, *Holy Things: A Liturgical Theology* (Minneapolis: Fortress Press, 1993), 119.

5. Martin Luther King Jr., "Letter from Birmingham Jail," April 16, 1963, http://okra.stanford.edu/transcription/document_images /undecided/630416-019.pdf.

6. Aidan Kavanagh, "Seeing Liturgically," in *Time and Community*, ed. J. Neil Alexander (Chicago: The Pastoral Press, 1990), 275.

7. Francis, *Evangelii Gaudium*, November 24, 2018, II.28, https://www.vatican.va/content/francesco/en/apost_exhortations /documents/papa-francesco_esortazione-ap_20131124_evangelii -gaudium.html.

www.ingramcontent.com/pod-product-compliance
Lightning Source LLC
Chambersburg PA
CBHW030720110325
23287CB00002B/4